Tony Harrison

PLAYS SIX

Tony Harrison was born in Leeds in 1937. His volumes of poetry include *The Loiners* (winner of the Geoffrey Faber Memorial Prize), *Continuous, v.* (broadcast on Channel 4 in 1987, winning the Royal Television Society Award), *The Gaze of the Gorgon* (winner of the Whitbread Prize for Poetry) and *Laureate's Block*. Recognised as Britain's leading theatre and film poet, Tony Harrison has written extensively for the National Theatre, the New York Metropolitan Opera, the BBC, Channel 4, the RSC, and for unique ancient spaces in Greece, Austria and Japan. His films include *Black Daisies for the Bride*, which won the Prix Italia, *The Shadow of Hiroshima*, *Prometheus* and *Crossings*. Six volumes of plays, *Collected Film Poetry* and *The Inky Digit of Defiance: Selected Prose 1966–2016* are published by Faber and his *Collected Poems* by Penguin. His play *Fram* premiered at the National Theatre in 2008. Tony Harrison was awarded the PEN/Pinter Prize 2009, the European Prize for Literature 2010, the David Cohen Prize for Literature 2015, and the Premio Feronia 2016 in Rome, in special recognition of a foreign author.

T0333458

TONY HARRISON

Plays Six

Hecuba
with an introduction by the author

Fram

Iphigenia in Crimea

Foreword by Lee Hall

ff

FABER & FABER

This collection first published in 2019
by Faber and Faber Limited
74–77 Great Russell Street
London WC1B 3DA

Typeset by Country Setting, Kingsdown, Kent CT14 8ES
Printed in England by CPI Group (UK) Ltd, Croydon CR0 4YY

Hecuba © Tony Harrison, 2005
Fram © Tony Harrison, 2008
Iphigenia in Crimea © Tony Harrison, 2016

Foreword © Lee Hall, 2017
First published in *New Light on Tony Harrison*
for the British Academy by OUP, 2019

A CIP record for this book is available from the British Library

978–0–571–35252–4

2 4 6 8 10 9 7 5 3 1

Contents

Foreword
by Lee Hall

THE MAN WHO CAME TO READ THE METRE

In the early 1980s, when I was a teenager growing up in Newcastle, I had a girlfriend who one Christmas Eve announced that I had to be at her house the next morning as a man would come, have a glass of hock, and recite excerpts from 'The Lady of Shalott' to the tune of 'When I'm Cleaning Windows'. Apparently this happened every Christmas and was something I couldn't afford to miss.

So on Christmas morning I duly made my way to the leafy part of town and sure enough around eleven o'clock a man arrived – downed a glass of German wine – and I waited – and I waited – but he didn't do it! He just talked – about food, wine, literature and theatre. He had apparently just come back from Greece or somewhere.

He had an open-necked shirt and a knotted kerchief around his neck. And thus he was, definitively, the most bohemian person I had ever seen. And by far the most cultured. Somehow I think I expected a poet to be more fusty – but there he was: at ease, worldly, confident, funny, learned; and I quailed in the corner, terrified I'd be asked a question – waiting for Tennyson in 4/4 time.

After about an hour he left on his rounds – without having done it! But I did not go home disappointed. I may not have heard the one-man Tennyson/Formby mash-up but I had had my first glimpse of Tony Harrison.

After that Christmas morning he seemed to be every-where. Not in person, you understand. But in the 1980s you couldn't get away from him. There were poems on telly, *The Mysteries* were at the National Theatre, *Selected Poems* came out in a Penguin paperback. I'd missed the *Oresteia* but my drama teacher had the video – which we all watched several times. I'd turn on the telly and there he was singing the virtues of Robert Service, next he'd be on *The South Bank Show* reading from his sonnets. A torrent of creativity, formidable in its breadth; vital, ambitious, relevant. It was a remarkable time for me, taking all this in.

And, of course, it must have been a remarkable time for Tony. I think only Yeats and Eliot in the twentieth century have had a decade like it, where their theatre work and their poetry had such a platform, was being created at such a pitch, being heard, understood and absorbed.

It was certainly manna to me and, like so many of my generation, I lapped it up. Our paths did not cross again for thirty years, but Tony Harrison became my hero.

Of course the sonnets about his parents – and the rupture that poetry and education had in terms of class – seemed to speak to me directly. I was the first person in our family to stay at school beyond fifteen, and already the dislocations that he wrote about were impinging on my own life.

But I think it was his writing for the theatre that was so overwhelming. Of course I read what I could of Tony's work. But it was seeing *The Mysteries* on telly one Christmas that really affected me. I think it must have been 1985. I sat up and watched it alone because no one else wanted to sit through seven hours of 'theatre'. I watched and wept. God spoke to me in the vernacular. I had never seen anything that matched its invention, its scope, the sheer fun, the vigour, warmth, intelligence, and I sat alone that night shaking because I knew that's what I had to do with my life.

Fuelled by all of this, I somehow managed to get myself into Cambridge to study English Literature. I remember arriving on the first day to find my posh girlfriend had sent a package to my pigeonhole. It was a fresh copy of *v*. So my first memory of Cambridge is sitting on the college lawn reading Tony's poem about a fractured nation. The devastated Northern Coalfield felt very far away from those hallowed halls. Yet it was a moment of great excitement for me. And also, of course, one of extreme dislocation. Not exactly helped by that particular meditation. But I did understand that Tony was my guide and I knew the point of being there was to try to make art out of it. And though it took the best part of decade to find its final shape, it was the moment *Billy Elliot* was born.

The fact that Tony was born in 1937 meant he was eight when the 'Butler' Education Act 1944 came into effect. So perhaps, if he'd been conceived just three years earlier, he would have not sat the Eleven Plus, and therefore not gone to Leeds Grammar School. He would not have been pilloried for his working-class accent and refused the right to speak the poems of (of all people, the hostler's son) Keats. But by being born exactly when he was, he did end up there, and so became one of the first of a cohort whose lives were upended by simply doing what you were expected to do at school.

What you were taught at Leeds Grammar was not what you were habitually taught in Beeston. Just by following the basic curriculum, the working-class kid enters a brave new world and the person he is most amazed to find in it is himself. The study of the Classics, or of literature, is therefore not simply the vehicle which will transport him out of his class. It is fundamentally transformative. It becomes the very roots of your identity. For him to follow literature is not indulging a penchant for the arts instead of a natural route into a profession or the City. It is his very being. This seems evident in every line Tony's written.

'I wanted to make poetry a real job', he has said, 'and that's a question of hazarding your whole life on what you do.' [1] Poetry or bust. I think that's what's so dramatic about Tony's writing: the stakes really are that high.

Yet the question of legitimacy seems to haunt the working-class artist. Despite the determined labour that is required in any scholarship, somehow it still seems high falutin. How can it earn its keep in a world of people who make things – by hard graft?

'Art as work' and the 'work of art' are immediate problems for anyone who was not born into culture. Art, for them, is not transparent. It is opaque with contradiction because of what (and whom) it excludes. And it's what I find so powerfully expressed in all Tony's work: the clear-sightedness that however conciliatory poetry is (i.e. implicitly unifying through the translation of experience), he consistently acknowledges it is always at the same time a document of some kind of barbarism.

The thing is, the scholarship boy takes his learning seriously. It represents not only all he has but everything he's given up to get it. And if he is to take the injunction of this education seriously – if he has taken the Greeks to heart – he understands he is required to use poetry to disrupt as much as to console. And that if it is to be serious it has also to be fun.

Yet he feels it is not enough simply to entertain or *épater le bourgeois*. Something more is at stake:

I came from a loving, rooted upbringing which was disrupted by Education and Poetry. And I've been trying to create new wholes out of that disruption ever since.[2]

Tony's answer to the problem has been to create a reflexive art which admits and examines this complexity – and a crucial part of the work is to address people directly. Personal tribulations are afforded legitimacy by making them, as he calls it, a 'public poetry'; that is, a poetry that is not simply individually consumed but is communally shared.

One only has to hear Tony read to understand how important this is. But what is so singular is his pursuit of this into unchartered waters, such as in the magnificent series of films on the telly. But as groundbreaking and innovative as these film-poems were, I think it's in theatre where he has really made this work most profoundly.

Verse drama seemed to have died a death, it is safe to say, with Christopher Fry, but the triumph of his *Misanthrope* led Tony to be the de facto writer-in-residence at the National Theatre through the whole of the 1970s and 1980s. It was an exceptional position for a poet to find themselves in, and one might have expected him to dust off a few more canonical favourites and apply his coruscating couplets.

But Tony took the job very seriously, tracing poetry and theatre to a common root which led him to two foundational texts – to the oldest play in the Western canon: the *Oresteia* of Aeschylus; and the English mystery plays which are the bedrock of all English drama. Both of these play cycles were central to the civic life of the societies in which they were performed. The *Oresteia* is in many ways *about* the creation of a civil order and the mystery plays embody the broadest sense of a demotic theatre. They were made by, and performed to, ordinary working folk via the guilds and were obviously central to the life of the medieval towns from which they emerged.

These are sprawling works, often deemed recondite and obscure, and because of their size and obscurity had remained largely aloof from popular production – if they were performed at all it was largely as academic or 'heritage' performances. But Tony understood that these plays presented a platform for the direct, democratic, 'public' theatre he'd been looking for. He grasped that the poetry of this theatre was not just in the language; it was in the contract it made with the audience. They were to be addressed eye to eye. He understood why it had to be in verse. Not only that, he understood how to do it. Not just because he was an accomplished poet and classical scholar. He understood because he had seen the last days of variety in Leeds, which addressed the audience directly and paid no heed to a fourth wall.

I like to think he understood the practical mechanics of such a theatre because when he got to Leeds University he was in a revue with (improbably) both Wole Soyinka and Barry Cryer.

He took the detail of these plays seriously. He didn't 'do a version' of the Greek plays like, say, Sartre. He understood that the actual words mattered, that these weren't precious pieces of arcana; these were where the roots of culture were buried and they were exhilarating, accessible, democratic works that made soaring poetry out of rough speech. Both of these works did on a vast scale what his poems did intimately: they were civilising, ultimately comedic in their structure, opening out on to fields of hope yet unafraid to broach difficult things, in difficult times.

Batter, batter the doom-drum, but believe there'll be better![3]

Pessimism of the intellect. Optimism of the will.

Famously, Tony brushed aside questions of the enormous work that was involved in shaping the mystery cycle by claiming he just 'came in to read the metre'.[4] It is indeed something he has done often: reading Aeschylus through the Gawain poet, football chants through Thomas Gray (even if he failed to do it that Christmas for Tennyson via Formby).

But what struck me recently when thinking about this off-the-cuff remark was that behind the image of the meter reader is an evocation of a time when we had public utilities that needed tending. Tony was there at the advent of our National Theatre. It was a time when the train you sat on to get there, the water you got at the bar, the electricity that provided the illumination was all publicly owned. Was all held in common.

And in that moment so was culture.

The *Oresteia* was directed by a stationmaster's son from Suffolk (Peter Hall), the music composed by a baker's son from Accrington (Harrison Birtwistle), *The Mysteries* were directed by a shipyard worker's son from Greenock (Bill Bryden). The companies were full of folk for whom RP was a foreign language. In terms of class, at least, it was a National Theatre.

Tony held us all in common. He understood that the gods speak in dialect at the National Theatre. That you could think about your mam and dad in Meredithian sonnets. He understood that plays could be poetical, that

verse could be foul-mouthed and outspoken without com-
promising a jot of its seriousness.

The gesture of turning the satyrs of Oxyrhynchus into
the poor souls of Cardboard City, the people excluded from
society, never mind high art, was a theatrical moment I will
never forget. I don't think an audience at the National has
ever been so profoundly challenged. We'd passed those very
people on our way in. It was chilling and heartbreaking.

That clog-dancing led very directly to the idea of trans-
posing the Billy Elliot story to the stage as a grand variety
show. Tell the story using 'our culture', Tony seemed to be
saying.

As the last two decades have shown, Tony is much more
than just a writer. He invents a *production* and not just
what goes on stage. He imagines what it will be like to
watch it. He sees the event in the round. And I think this
is where his influence is most keenly felt. Not on writers,
who, to be quite frank, don't have the technical apparatus
to properly follow in his footsteps, but a generation of
directors and theatre-makers saw that work and were profoundly changed by it.

They are a generation of theatre-makers who take it as
read that the text and the theatrical gesture should be in-
extricably intertwined, that we can forgo naturalism but
lose none of our intimacy or the grain of spoken language,
that a satyr is just as important as a saint, that in art the con-
frontational is also a form of consolation, and very often
vice versa. I am thinking of people like Simon McBurney
from Complicite, Emma Rice of Kneehigh, Declan Don-
nellan of Cheek by Jowl and many, many more.

Dominic Dromgoole summed it up for my generation
in the year 2000 when he said that Tony Harrison was 'the
vernacular virtuoso behind three of the greatest theatrical
events of the last thirty years: the *Oresteia, The Mysteries*
and *The Trackers of Oxyrhynchus*'.[5] These are monu-
mental achievements. I think of what Basil Bunting said
about Pound's *Cantos*: 'Here are the Alps. You will have

to go a long way round if you want to avoid them.'[6] Since then Tony has continued to write and direct a series of plays in verse that have no equal. They are unlike anybody else's, yet they are full of ideas, spectacle and a celebration of language which goes to the root of all important theatre.

And it's this call to a 'public poetry' through the theatre that I think a generation of mavericks has taken up. So Tony's more recent work has much more in common with the kids who are trying to make unofficial theatre outside the tradition of the 'well-made play' than it does with the accomplished playwrights on the boulevards of the South Bank.

It would be remiss not to worry about the Tony Harrisons of the future. I am not advocating the return of grammar schools, but it seems clear to me that people like Tony or myself are getting thinner on the ground. It is hard to hear those working-class voices. And it's the high arts that suffer for it. That's why Tony's example is so important.

For my own part, I don't think I've written a sentence without thinking 'Oh God, Tony Harrison could do this better, and in verse!' But it is because of Tony that I keep on having a go. My literary hero at seventeen, my literary hero at fifty. An immense thank you.

1. Quoted in P. Forbes, 'In the Canon's Mouth', in S. Byrne, ed., *Tony Harrison and the Classics* (forthcoming), p. 193.

2. J. Haffenden, 'Interview with Tony Harrison', in N. Astley, ed., *Bloodaxe Critical Anthology 1: Tony Harrison* (Newcastle upon Tyne: Bloodaxe Books, 1991), p. 246.

3. Aeschylus, *Agamemnon,* line 159 in Harrison's translation.

4. This was how Harrison introduced himself when interviewed by Melvyn Bragg on the *South Bank Show* in 1980.

5. Dominic Dromgoole, *The Full Room* (London: Methuen, 2000), p. 134.

6. B. Bunting, *Descant on Rawthey's Madrigal: Conversations with Basil Bunting* (Lexington KY: Gnomon Press, 1968), p. 110.

Delivered at 'New Light on Tony Harrison', a conference convened by Professor Edith Hall and hosted by the British Academy, 27–28 April 2017, to celebrate the poet's eightieth birthday.

HECUBA

of Euripides

Weeping for Hecuba

What's Hecuba to him, or he to Hecuba,
That he should weep for her?
Hamlet, Act II, Scene 2

Though no doubt the original Athenian audiences wept for Hecuba in the two plays of Euripides in which she is the principal figure – *Hecuba* of about 423 BC and *The Trojan Women* of 415 BC – the first named person we know who wept for Hecuba was a notoriously cruel tyrant, Alexander of Pherae, in the fourth century BC, and he was ashamed of it. Plutarch tells his story in two versions, and in one it seems that the monster shed tears at a performance of *The Trojan Women* and in the other at a performance of *Hecuba*. The tyrant was so moved to pity by the spectacle of the Queen of Troy, without husband, sons or city, reduced to slavery, that he jumped up and ran from the theatre as fast as he could. He said it would be terrible if when he was killing so many of his own subjects he should be seen to be shedding tears over the sufferings of Hecuba and Polyxena, the daughter of Hecuba sacrificed after the Trojan War was over to appease the ghost of Achilles. Alexander the tyrant almost had the actor who played Hecuba severely punished for having softened his heart 'like iron in the furnace'.

What the man of iron had been surprised by was that bond of empathy and compassion that can cross centuries, and which, along with the imagination that needs to be primed to experience both, was dangerously undermining for the tyranny and oppression that upheld Alexander's power. Oppression and empathy can't co-exist.

In these two plays of Euripides, set in the immediate aftermath of the Trojan War, the poet creates one of the great archetypes of suffering. For an actress it is a role of the tragic grandeur of Lear, except that for the Queen of Troy the play begins by cutting straight to Shakespeare's Act III, the storm and the heath – and the sense of total deprivation. Hecuba enters deprived of everything she had – husband, sons, city, wealth, status – reduced to ending her days as a Greek slave scrubbing Agamemnon's latrines.

This reversal of fortune was the theme that appealed to the earliest appreciators of *Hecuba* in the sixteenth century, when it was translated from Greek into the more accessible Latin by Erasmus and Philip Melanchthon, who put on his version acted by students of his university at Wittenberg, where Hamlet was said to have studied.

The other theme was revenge; though it is a strange play about revenge that begins with the ghost of a murdered Trojan boy asking simply for burial and a last embrace from his mother, Hecuba. But he also tells us of another, angrier, unresigned ghost: that of Achilles, who can't rest without the shedding of more innocent blood. We are encouraged to cheer Hecuba on to her revenge against Polymestor, who has murdered her son Polydorus for gold, though we are chilled by the action when it happens. Euripides never makes it easy for us, tears or no tears.

It took the twentieth century's horrors and the rediscovery of *The Trojan Women* to turn the moralist of fate and the vicissitudes of fortune into an almost modern political playwright. Once discovered, it revealed that *Hecuba* was about the corruption of both power and powerlessness. The range of compromised violence it covers, even from a distance of twenty-five centuries, is from computerised aerial bombardment to the suicide bomber.

Three months after Franz Werfel, the Austrian poet and dramatist, translated *The Trojan Women* in 1914, the Serbian nationalist Princip assassinated Franz Ferdinand in Sarajevo. Werfel had written prophetically in his preface to his version of Euripides: 'Tragedy and hapless Hecuba may now return; their time has come.' In fact Hecuba's time had already come at the beginning of the century, since when her glaring spotlight has never been dimmed. Gilbert Murray, the great humanist, early idealist of the League of Nations, and (despite the later rejection of his Swinburnian poetic ear) the great populariser of Greek drama, did a version of the same *Trojan Women* which Harley Granville Barker, who was responsible for ground-breaking productions of Greek tragedy, directed at the Royal Court Theatre in 1905.

The production was seen as 'pro-Boer'. Murray was outspoken in his opposition to the Boer War. He saw inevitable parallels between the suffering of Hecuba and the women of Troy and the Boer women and children whose homesteads were burnt to the ground and who were interned by Lord Kitchener in concentration camps – a phrase coined then to describe this British invention. The Edwardians were made to squirm uncomfortably with guilt at the obvious similarities between Greek and British imperialism. Euripides no doubt deliberately made his own audience squirm when in an almost blasphemous parody of a democratic process he shows the assembled coalition army debating whether to sacrifice Polyxena, the daughter of Hecuba. The principal proposers of the motion are the two sons of Theseus, Athenians. He also allows Odysseus, the 'molasses-mouth' master of spin, to win over the coalition vote for sacrificing an innocent girl.

The girl, Polyxena, is to be sacrificed to the ghost of Achilles by Achilles' son, the notoriously psychotic Arkan-like Neoptolemus. Neoptolemus' notoriety is given graphic detail on some extant vases. On a red-figure vase in the Archaeological Museum of Naples, Neoptolemus is shown savagely hacking at the old King Priam, the husband of Hecuba, who has their grandson on his knees. also hacked to death. There are numerous slashes and gashes on the body of the child and on the old man's head, to show the fury of the assault. On a cup in the Louvre, Neoptolemus is shown braining Priam with the hacked body of his dead grandson. He is also shown, nearer home in the British Museum, sticking his sword into the gullet of Polyxena, who is held over the sacrificial tomb by three soldiers. It is one of the most brutal of amphorae. It makes us think of Nietszche's description of the Greeks as 'civilised savages'.

Euripides knows the track record of Neoptolemus but he deliberately gives us another version, which shows him moved for a moment, like Alexander. Pity wells up in him and has to be suppressed. The coalitions's messenger Talthybius, who goes further and weeps for the daughter of Hecuba, in a great descriptive speech tells how Polyxena requests that no one should restrain her and that she will die 'free'. He describes her being lifted onto the tomb like a stage from which she makes her speech and then, of her own will, rips open her robe, baring her breast and throat to the executioner's sword-thrust. Even the compulsively vicious Neoptolemus is impressed by the bravery of the victim's performance and for an instant holds back his sword. But only for an instant. There are empathetic tears in the Greek coalition ranks and they throw tokens of regard on the body of the girl, though they'd roared assent at the decision to sacrifice an innocent. Behind it also lies Euripides' questioning of the use of tears, and by implication of tragic drama itself, at a time when Athens was in the process of a bloody and ultimately self-destructive war. Or at any time since for that matter.

In my notebooks, where I glue pictures among the drafts of translations from the Greek tragedies I've done, I have a recurring image of an old woman appealing to the camera that has captured her agony or the heavens that ignore it, in front of the utter devastation that had been her home, or before her murdered dead. They are all different women from many places on earth with the same gesture of disbelief, despair and denunciation. They are in

Sarajevo, Kosovo, Grozny, Gaza, Ramallah, Tblisi, Baghdad, Falluja: women in robes and men in hard metal helmets, as in the Trojan War. Under them all, over the years, I have scribbled Hecuba. My notebooks are bursting with Hecubas. Hecuba walks out of Eurpides from two thousand five hundred years ago straight onto our daily front pages and into our nightly newscasts. She is never out of the news. To our shame she is news that stays news.

When Granville Barker took Gilbert Murray's version of *The Trojan Women* to New York in May 1915 and played in the Adolph Lewisohn Stadium, an effort was made to persuade President Woodrow Wilson to write a special preface to the published text, but he replied that that he must 'detach himself from everything which seems to bear the character of an attempt to make opinion even in the interest of peace'. I wonder what President Bush would reply if the RSC asked him to write a preface to my version of *Hecuba* to coincide with its visit to the Kennedy Center in Washington. And would he weep for Vanessa Redgrave's Hecuba if he could be somehow tricked into attending a performance?

At the end of the First World War, in 1919, Sybil Thorndike played Hecuba at the Old Vic, in order to raise funds for the newly founded League of Nations (Gilbert Murray was the chairman of the League of Nations Union). She tells of a tough cockney barrow-woman saying to her, 'Well, dearie, we saw your play . . . and we all 'ad a good cry – you see, them Trojans was just like us, we've lost our boys in this war, 'aven't we, so no wonder we was all cryin' – that was a real play, that was, dearie.' Sybil Thorndike remembers a later performance at the Alhambra Theatre in Leicester Square as the most moving she could ever remember: 'All the misery and awfulness of the 1914 war was symbolised in that play, and we all felt here was the beginning of a new era of peace and brotherhood.'

Many had a good cry, but the League that Hecuba's tragic fate raised funds for didn't prevent the Second World War, and the four Doric columns used in this setting for the sufferings of Sybil Thorndike's Hecuba were destroyed in a German bombing raid on the RADA theatre in the London Blitz. Nor did the UN, the institution that succeeded the League, manage to prevent the 'coalition' invading Iraq. We may still be weeping for Hecuba, but we allow our politicians to flood the streets of Iraq with more and more Hecubas in the name of freedom and democracy. The audience might weep for Hecuba in Washington when the tragedy plays there, but will they squirm with regret for Iraq, or the re-election of George Bush, or pause a moment before going for the gullet of Iran?

T.H.
Newcastle-upon-Tyne, February 2005

Hecuba in this new translation was first presented by the Royal Shakespeare Company at the Albery Theatre, London, on 26 March 2005. The cast was as follows:

The Ghost of Polydorus Matthew Douglas
Hecuba Vanessa Redgrave
Polyxena Lydia Leonard
Odysseus Darrell D'Silva
Talthybius Alan Dobie
Agamemnon Malcolm Tierney
Polymestor Darrell D'Silva
Guards Christopher Terry, Matthew Douglas
Servant Judith Paris
Chorus Charlotte Allam, Jane Arden, Rosalie Craig, Maisie Dimbleby, Barbara Gellhorn, Aileen Gonsalves, Michele Moran, Sasha Oakley, Katherine O'Shea, Judith Paris, Sarah Quist, Natalie Turner-Jones

Director Laurence Boswell
Designer Es Devlin
Lighting Adam Silverman
Sound Mic Pool
Music Mick Sands
Movement Gary Sefton
Choreography Heather Habens

Characters

The Ghost of Polydorus
Hecuba
Polyxena
Odysseus
Talthybius
Agamemnon
Polymestor
Servant
Chorus

THE GHOST OF POLYDORUS

Those dark cells where all the dead are held
behind gloom's gates where Hades scorns the gods
and skulks apart. This ghost here's come from there.
I was Polydorus, Hecuba and Priam's son.
My father Priam fearing Troy would fall
had a foreboding that we'd end up occupied
by the Greek coalition and so had me sent
secretly from Troy where I'd be safe
with Polymestor, Father's Thracian friend,
who farms these fertile flatlands of the Chersonese
and rules his horsemen folk with iron force.
With me he sent a hush-hush stash of gold
so if Troy fell his sons could still survive.
Too weedy of muscle to wield a man's shield,
the runt of the litter, I was smuggled out,
and while Troy's boundaries were still intact,
her turrets and her towers not yet toppled,
and brother Hector still lucky in combat,
under the care of my father's Thracian friend,
I blossomed, though was soon to be blasted.
Once Hector, the soul of Troy, was stricken,
my father's sanctuaries all razed and gutted,
the king himself hacked down while he clung
to the most sacred shrine in all of Troy,
butchered by that brute Neoptolemus,
the blood-sodden son of Achilles,
my father's friend killed me to get my gold
and slung my slashed-up corpse into the swell
and gloated on the gold now in his grasp.

Sometimes sprawled on sand and sometimes spume
my corpse bobs on the ebb, and then gets pushed
by the brash thrust of the flow back on the shore,
unbewailed and unburied. So now I hover
over my dear mother, Hecuba, a ghost,
my body's void shell bobbing on the swell.
I've been hovering above for three days now
as long as my poor mother brought from Troy
's been captive in this place, the Chersonese.
The Greeks are camping near their anchored ships
in enforced idleness on these shores of Thrace
because Achilles rose out of his tomb
and stopped the whole Greek coalition force
weighing anchor and unfurling sails
and pulling on their oars straight back for home.
His phantom craves my sister for his grave,
Polyxena, the blood-grace due his ghost.
He'll get what he demands, not go without
the accolade of comrades and close friends.
My sister will meet her fate this very day,
the day my mother will be forced to see
two of her children dead. Polyxena. And me.
To get my burial I'll reveal myself
where the waves break at a woman's feet.
I prised this promise from the powers below
begging a mother's burial, a last embrace.
All that I longed for will be given me.

That's her, Hecuba, my mother, coming now
from the tent where Agamemnon keeps his slaves.
I'll withdraw. She dreams of me. She's scared.

Aaaaahhhh!
Poor mother, once a queen and now a slave.
Your old well-being balanced now by bale.
He heaps woes in the scales, some god or other.
Those woes weigh more than joys did, O poor mother!

Exit Ghost of Polydorus.

HECUBA

Someone help. Anyone,
one of you Trojan girls,
to bring the old woman out,
out of her lodgings
and see I don't stumble.
I may well be a slave
along with all of you,
but I *was* a queen, once,
so keep my back upright.
Some crooked arm for comfort,
for support as my stave,
as the old bones try bustling
with a pace past their power.

Bright sunflash of Zeus,
night with your darkness,
I'm terrified by fears
and night phantoms. Why?

Earth, who gives birth
to dreams with black wings,
I refuse to believe
that night vision's true.
Gods underground
keep my son safe!
He's my one anchor left.
He's hereabouts
in snowswept Thrace,
safe in the hands
of his father's friend.

More bad's bound to happen!
More lamenting, more keening
for women keened dry.
More weeping for red eyes

whose tear-ducts are drained.
My heart's never before
been so full of dark shudders.
I can't stop it shivering.
My fear-gripped flesh flutters.
I need my prophetic children,
Helenus or Cassandra.
They'd know what these dreams mean.

CHORUS

Hecuba, Hecuba,
I wanted to come to you
as soon as you called
but it's only now I've been able
to sneak from my master's tent,
the master who won me
at the slave allocation
of us women all driven
out of Ilium's city,
hunted and herded at spearpoint,
slaves, drudges, chattels,
for the conquering Greeks.

Your grief load, though,
I can't make it lighter.
The message I'm bringing
means burdens more massive.
I'm a herald of horrors:

The whole Achaean coalition
in full council cast its vote
to dedicate your daughter
as Achilles' sacrifice.
You know that the ghost of Achilles
hovered over his grave-mound.
Gleaming in gold war-gear
he halted the sea-borne Achaean fleet.

As the sailors wound in the cables
his ghost barked at the Greeks:

Where are you off to
you Greeks in a hurry
grudging my grave-mound
the giftright it's due?

What followed after
was will-clash and conflict
welling and surging
through the whole summoned army,
opinions splintering
the spear-coalition,
some for the sacrifice
and others against.
King Agamemnon, though,
spoke up on your side,
through care for Cassandra,
your daughter possessed
of prophetess power,
the king's concubine.
The sons of Theseus
both bred in Athens,
made separate speeches
but were of the same mind,
that the grave-mound of Achilles
be given its crown of glory,
a fresh gore garland
from a green girl.
They weren't the kind,
so they claimed, to set
Cassandra's cuddles
above the claims of Achilles
with all his kudos from combat.

The passions on both sides
were in some sort of stalemate,

the debate in a deadlock,
till hair-splitter, shifty-wits,
molasses-mouth, mob-schmoozer
Odysseus won the ranks over,
persuading them not to spurn
the ace of the whole coalition,
just to spare the life of some slave.
How could they ever confront
the Queen of the Underworld
when they died and confess
Greek ingratitude was such
that they quit the plains of Troy
without first placating
the spirit of those fallen
in defence of their comrades?
Any minute now he'll be here
will Odysseus to grab
your little cub from your bosom,
bundle your baby off
from your feeble embrace.
The only hope left to you
is in altars and temples
(though you won't find them here),
or grasping his knees
to beg Agamemnon.
Pray to anything at all
the sky god, the earth god.
If no prayers can prevent
you losing your daughter,
you'll see your girl sprawled
on the great hero's grave-mound,
a glow of gore around her neck
bridal gold not bloodfleck beads should deck.

HECUBA

Can't cry! Can't keen!
A slave's foul suffering,

foul age don't make you sing,
voice and freedom gone.
Who else could endure
disasters so dire?

Who'll be my shield and defender?
No city, no surviving kin,
my dear husband dead and gone,
my sons all six feet under.
All routes out a blocked dead end
unless some god turns out a friend.

Women, who've suffered as I have,
the bad news that you've brought
destroys me. I'm destroyed.
I'll be glad to get into my grave.
My life's all over. It's done
There's no joy for me in the sun.

Come on, old creaky-bones,
get the queen to her 'palace' door.
Your mother's suffering's been dire
and you're the heiress to my pains.
The most luckless woman on this earth
gave you your unlucky birth.

Polyxena!

POLYXENA

It must be something really bad.
It must be unendurable news
for you to make that moaning noise
that panics your little bird.

HECUBA

O my little child, *omoi, omoi*!

POLYXENA

The way your voice sounds frightens me.
It must mean something really bad.

HECUBA

Your life, poor innocent wretch.

POLYXENA

Tell it to me straight. Don't hedge.
I'm scared of what your groans forebode.

HECUBA

Bad luck's in your blood. My child! My child!

POLYXENA

The news and nothing more. I must be told.

HECUBA

It's you! Achilles' sacrifice.
The army's voted you'll be killed
on the tomb of Achilles. My poor child,
you're to be the phantom's prize.

POLYXENA

What are you saying? No! They can't.
Mother, Mother, I don't understand.

HECUBA

The army voted, and the vote
decreed they'd cut your throat.

POLYXENA

No one's life's been more ill-starred!
No one's suffered more than you,
no one, no one, now come new
atrocities some demon's stirred.

No more, no more, now frail and old
can you lean on your loving child.

Mother, Mother, what makes me sad
's you'll lack the love and the support
of me, your loyal little bird,
enduring slavery by your side.

HECUBA

Now you'll have to watch men grab
your uncoralled and crag-bred cub.

You'll have to watch it happen
being torn from your loving hug,
sacrificed, spreadeagled, struck,
my girl's gullet gashed open,
despatched down to the world below
where dead Polyxena will lie.

CHORUS

Hecuba, look, there's Odysseus approaching
in a hurry to pass on the new declaration.

ODYSSEUS

Madam, I imagine you've been made aware
how the army's minded and their vote was cast
and how the coalition ballot was concluded
but I'll spin through it again so we're all clear.
The coalition vote elects your daughter
as the dedication for Achilles' tomb.
We're here to take charge of and escort the girl.
The son of Achilles, Neoptolemus,
will preside as the priest and despatcher.
You know the form. Don't force us to use force
and pull the girl roughly out of your clutches.
No one wants to watch you wrestling me.
Best assess your strength and situation.
Slaves don't have any choice. Be sensible.

HECUBA
(aside)

Ahhhh!
I'm in for a struggle or so it seems,
one that may end in keening and tears.
I should've died the day that Priam died.
Now I know why Zeus wanted me to live.
Instead of grinding me into the grave
Zeus grooms me for more grief, only grimmer!

(To Odysseus.)
If it's permitted for mere slaves to pose
questions to a free man of the kind
that aren't contentious or provocative,
permit me now to pose a few to you.
Then I'll listen carefully to your response.

ODYSSEUS
I'll make this one exception in your case.

HECUBA
Remember when you came to spy on Troy?
In ugly disguise and disreputable rags.
Blood dribbled from your eyes down to your chin.

ODYSSEUS
It's deep in my memory. Too deeply in!

HECUBA
Helen recognised you. Only I was told.

ODYSSEUS
I remember the danger. My blood ran cold.

HECUBA
You clasped my knees in desperate suppliant's grip.

ODYSSEUS
I got white knuckles clutching at your robe.

HECUBA
You were my slave. What did you say to me?

ODYSSEUS
O anything to make you set me free.

HECUBA
I let you go. I let you get away.

ODYSSEUS
Which is why I still look on the light of day.

HECUBA

Then don't you feel begrimed by how you act?
You acknowledge you had benefits from me
yet instead of good you only do me harm.
What a graceless breed you are, you demagogues,
grubbing for favours from the mob. Spare me your
    friendship.
You'd harm your friends if that would please the mob.
Why do they think themselves so full of wisdom,
voting for the death of my poor girl?
Does something force them into human sacrifice?
Heifers not humans are fit offerings for tombs.
If Achilles wants retaliation and revenge
why Polyxena? She did no harm to him.
Helen's the better victim for his ghost.
Her fault he came to Troy. She sealed his doom.
If beauty's wanted in the one who dies
none of us slaves are beautiful enough.
Helen's most outstanding for her looks
and her guilt's more than ours could ever be.
Simple justice is behind my plea.
Listen to what I feel that you owe me.
I showed you mercy once. Now pay me back.
As you confessed, you fell down at my feet.
You grasped my hand. You touched my wrinkled cheek.
Now I do the same to you, and humbly beg
you show the same compassion I showed you.
Don't tear my little child out of my arms.
Don't kill her. Thousands are already dead.
The powerful shouldn't let their power corrupt.
And the lucky shouldn't think luck lasts for good.
Once I had luck, but haven't any now.
One day is all it takes to change all that.
I touch you on the chin, your suppliant.
Show me some respect and pity me.
Go back to your Greek army. Change their minds.

Warn them that retribution lies in wait
if they kill women whom at first they spared
when they dragged them off the shrine-stones where
    they clung.
You Greeks, you have a law on shedding blood.
It applies to free men and to slaves alike.
Your status counts for something with the Greeks
even when your arguments might not convince.
Where a nobody might fail, a man like you,
with reputation, makes the same speech work.

CHORUS

Can there be anyone with heart so hard,
who'd listen to such grief and not shed tears?

ODYSSEUS

Hecuba, let me give you some advice
and try not to resent it if I do.
For your past compassion to me I'm prepared
to spare your life. Believe me I'm sincere,
but I can't go back on what I told the troops
that now Troy's taken they should make your girl
the blood-gift to the army's leading light.
His ghost demands it and they owe him that.
It would be shameful, if we honour him
while he's alive, but once he's dead, we don't.
Suppose we have to mobilise again,
and we're mustering our forces and recruiting,
will men enlist, or want to save their skins,
when a fallen hero doesn't get his due
and soldiers give their lives and no one cares?
There's little that I want while I'm alive
but I want honour shown my tomb for all to see,
some posterity in public gratitude.

You say you're suffering. I say this in reply:
we've got old women and old men at home
who've suffered agonies no less than yours,

and young brides robbed of their young grooms
whose bodies lie yonder under Ida's dust.
You have to learn to put up with such things.
If our custom of giving honour to the dead's
wrong-headed, then I'm proud to say we're mad.
If barbarians like you betray your friends
and don't give honours to the glorious dead,
that benefits our side, and Greece prevails
and you reap the harvest of your scorn of friends.

CHORUS

Slavery's an evil, and will always be,
human beings brutalised by force.

HECUBA

(to Polyxena)

My words against your murder have misfired.
They've fallen wide of target, all no use.
If you've got powers greater than your mother
give fervent vent to all your vocal art,
and like the nightingale plead for your life.
Fall pathetically at Odysseus' knees.
Try to persuade him (he's a parent too!)
to take pity on your plight and spare your life.

POLYXENA

I see you, Odysseus, hiding your right hand
under your cloak. You turn your head away
so I can't touch your beard in supplication.
Don't be alarmed. I'm not a suppliant.
The suppliants' Zeus won't put you on the spot.
I'll go with you. But not because I must,
or because I'm now a slave and have no choice,
but of my own free will. I want to die.
If I weren't willing then I'd seem a coward,
a chicken-hearted clinger on to life.
What reason could I have to go on living?
Think how I started life, my father, king

of all the Phrygians and lord of Troy.
I was brought up to believe I'd be the bride
of some great king, and royal rivals vied
with each other to claim me for their bed.
I could have had my choice of any king.
A beggar now, I had at my beck and call
my Trojan women, but no man gazed
on any girl or woman more than me.
I'd almost seem divine but that I'd die.
Now I'm a slave. A slave! I never thought
a word so foreign could be used of me.
That, first and foremost, makes me want to die.
Suppose I end up owned by some crude brute
who'll pay some silver coins to purchase *me*,
the sister of Hector and heroic brothers,
made to knead dough in my master's kitchen,
scrub filthy floors, or labour at the loom,
forced, with no choice, on a treadmill of chores.
Some slave, bought who knows where, will foul my bed
considered once a fitter couch for kings.
No! My last look at the light of day
will be with eyes whose freedom's still undimmed.
I freely consign my corpse to those below.
Lead me off, Odysseus, lead me off.
I see nothing to give us hope, or a belief
that I ever have a chance of faring well.
Mother, say or do nothing to hinder them.
I beg you, Mother. Share my wish for death
before indignity or degradation.
Better off a corpse than live a slave.
Life without honour is a base ordeal.
Life's not worth living if it has no grace.

CHORUS

Breeding's a glorious carat-mark in men
but greater in the ones who've earned the stamp.

HECUBA

Nobly spoken, daughter, but so sad
in its nobility, so very sad.

(*To Odysseus.*)
If it's irreversible what's been decreed
in the matter of the blood-gift for the grave,
instead of risking guilt by killing her,
lead me to the pyre of Achilles, me.
Stab me! Show no mercy. I bore Paris
who killed Achilles with his sharp bow-shot.

ODYSSEUS

The ghost is craving younger blood than yours.

HECUBA

Then kill me alongside her so earth and ghost
get two good glugs of blood to glut their thirst.

ODYSSEUS

It's enough your daughter dies. No need to pile
death onto death. It pains me that there's one.

HECUBA

I demand my death the same time as my daughter's.

ODYSSEUS

Since when are you the one who gives the orders?

HECUBA

I'll cling to her like ivy clings round trees.

ODYSSEUS

Those with more sense will tell you it's no use.

HECUBA

I tell you that I'll keep her here with me.

ODYSSEUS

And I tell you when I leave so will she.

POLYXENA

Mother, listen! Son of Laertes, please
go easy on a parent understandably distressed.
Mother, don't struggle. They have all the power.
We don't want to see you flung down to the ground,
your delicate old skin all scratched and bruised
from being brutally manhandled. Don't!
It would be so unseemly to see you dragged
by some strong soldier. Don't! It's not dignified.
My darling mother give me your sweet hand
and let me put my cheek against your cheek.
For this one and final time, then never again
will I gaze on the sun's round orb and rays.
No more farewells. These are my last words.
Mother, Mother who bore me, now I go
to start my journey to the world below.

HECUBA

I pity you. Our suffering breaks my heart.

POLYXENA

I'll be in Hades. You here. Worlds apart.

HECUBA

I want to end my life. What can I do?

POLYXENA

Born free I was, but as a slave I'll die.

HECUBA

And I'll still be alive and still a slave.

POLYXENA

No wedding hymn, groomless, I go to my grave.

HECUBA

I had husband and family. Now nothing to show.

POLYXENA

Any words for Hector or your husband below?

HECUBA
Only how much I suffer without them up here.

POLYXENA
O bosom, I had such sweet suckling there.

HECUBA
O my daughter, my daughter, too young to die.

POLYXENA
Mother, farewell. Tell Cassandra goodbye.

HECUBA
Others may fare well, your mother no.

POLYXENA
Goodbye Polydorus, here in Thrace now.

HECUBA
If he's alive, which my luck makes me doubt.

POLYXENA
He'll be there to close your eyelids when you're dead.

HECUBA
I'm dead already though not yet in my grave.
I'm dead from too much suffering too much grief.

POLYXENA
Odysseus, let's go. Throw this cloak over me.
Even before I'm murdered, my heart melts
from my mother's keening; hers melts from mine.
Daylight, sun, I still can call your name
but only live one moment in your fire
before the sword-thrust at Achilles' pyre.

Exit Polyxena, led off by Odysseus.

HECUBA
Ah, I'm faint! My legs are giving way.
Daughter, reach out and touch me, stretch

your hand out so I can hold it. Don't,
don't leave me childless. I'm destroyed.

Hecuba collapses by the tent.

CHORUS

Ocean wind, ocean wind
wafting craft across the sea,
where will be my journey's end,
whose house-slave will I be?
Where in Greece will my ship land,
Argos, Sparta, Thessaly
where Apidanos floods the plain
keeping pastures plump with grain?

Or will swift oars that skim the foam
row me across to some small isle
to be shut away in some brute's home,
my slave's life, squalid, hard and vile,
or, to where the laurel and the palm
first grew to grace Leto's travail,
Delos, where, my best hope, this,
with virgins I'll hymn Artemis.

Or in Athens with the women weave
the saffron robe Athena wears.
With bright-hued threads and fine gold leaf
embroider on it her yoked mares,
or tableau where Zeus blasts his foes,
the Titans, with twin fire-bolt force.

Sons, husbands, brothers, fathers all
brained, stabbed or hacked to bits,
the city under a choking pall
of dustclouds from the Argive blitz.
We leave Asia to be Europe's slaves
in lands not chosen by ourselves.

Not like Polyxena in Hades, dead,
alive a slave in some Greek's bed.

Enter Talthybius.

TALTHYBIUS
Where can I find Hecuba once queen of Troy?

CHORUS
That's her there, Talthybius, full length,
flat on the ground, all bundled in her robes.

TALTHYBIUS
What is there to say? Does Zeus in fact
watch over men or is it all a tale?
Chance seems more in charge of men's affairs.
This, the Queen of Phrygia rich in gold?
This, the spouse of Priam, fortunate and blessed.
Now her city's utterly gutted by Greek force
and she's a childless old slave on the ground,
her poor old head and hair begrimed with muck.

I'm old myself but I'd prefer to croak
before I end up in a state like this.
Up you get, poor old soul. Try getting up.
Lift your old white head up off the ground.

HECUBA
Who's that won't let a poor soul lie in peace?
Whoever you are, just leave me to my grief.

TALTHYBIUS
It's Talthybius, Agamemnon's ADC,
sent by the army to have words with you.

HECUBA
I welcome you if your arrival means
the coalition wants me killed as well.
That's welcome news! O let's be off at once.
Take me to where they'll kill me, please, old man.

TALTHYBIUS
Lady, your daughter's dead, and I'm commanded
to escort you to attend to her last rites.

HECUBA

What are you saying? That you haven't come
to fetch me to be killed but bring bad news?
Dead, my darling, snatched from my embrace.
O yet another child I lose in you.
How did you do the deed? With some respect?
Or was she butchered like a hated foe?
Speak, though your words, I know, will break my heart.

TALTHYBIUS

You're asking me to weep a second time.
Telling the dreadful tale will make my eyes
well with the tears they welled with when she died.
The whole coalition force was standing by
around the tomb your girl was slaughtered on.
The son of Achilles took your daughter's hand
and stood her on the summit of the mound.
The crack Achaean guard stood by to curb
any frisky lurches from the skittish calf.
Then Neoptolemus, son of Achilles, took
a goblet of pure gold filled to the brim
in both his hands and raised it up aloft
as a drink-gift to his father's ghost.
He signalled me to call the men to order.
I took my stand among them and proclaimed
order and silence in all ranks. 'Order, order!'
Once I'd got total, breathless hush he spoke:

'Son of Peleus, Father, pray receive
these libations meant to charm the dead
and summon them from Hades to our world.
Come, drink this girl's dark undiluted blood
which the army and myself give as our gift.
We beg you for your blessing. Please allow
the fleet to weigh anchor and set sail for home
and find safe return back to the fatherland.'

He stopped. The whole massed army said *Amen*.

Then grasping his sword-hilt all inlaid with gold
he drew it from its sheath, and gave a nod
to the elite guard detailed to hold the girl.
Once she got wind of this she spoke these words:

'You Greeks who razed my city to the ground,
it's of my own free will that I die now.
I beg you don't restrain me when you strike
so, although I'll lose my life, I'll still be free.
My blood is royal and I couldn't bear
being branded as a slave among the dead.'
The men roared their assent and Agamemnon
commanded the chosen guard to let her go.
Once she'd heard her master's order to the men
she ripped her robe down from the collarbone
to a point at the midriff where the navel showed
and bared her breasts as beautiful as marble.
Then sinking to her knees onto the ground
she spoke the bravest words I've ever heard:
'Here, young man, if it's my breast you want,
strike here, if it's my neck, then here's my throat.'

Half-eager to do the deed, half-holding back
through pity for the girl, Achilles' son
sliced through her windpipe. Blood spurted out.
Though fading fast she still contrived to fall
with becoming modesty and so conceal
what should be hidden from the gaze of males.
Once she'd breathed her last from that death blow
the army took on tasks of various kinds.
Some covered the corpse by throwing leaves on her.
Others stacked up the pine-logs for the pyre.
Those who weren't busy were abused by those
who were, like this: 'Don't just stand there, oaf,
without something in your hands, some cloth, a brooch.
Find something to bestow on this brave girl
who showed more spirit than I've ever seen.'

That's your daughter's story. I'll say this:
you've got the best of children and the worst of fates.

CHORUS

Our city gutted, and our sons in graves.
The gods treat human beings like their slaves.

HECUBA

So many torments where shall I begin,
my daughter? When I try to deal with one
there's another that distracts me from the first
then yet another drawing me away,
grief always treading on the heels of grief.
I'll never wipe your death out of my mind.
I'll never cease to mourn it, but the news
you acted nobly slightly numbs the ache.
It's strange though, isn't it? How a poor soil
given good weather produces a good crop
while fertile soil that lacks the feed it needs
bears bad crops, but in the case of men
the bad man's never anything but bad,
the good man's good whatever blows he's dealt.

So my brain scatters its futile thoughts.

(To Talthybius.)

Please take a message to the Argive force.
Please let my daughter's body not be touched
and keep the curious crowd from round her corpse.
When you get men in their thousands under arms
they're prone to riot in the rank and file
and sailors go wild on land like forest fires.
They think you're crooked if you do no crimes.

Exit Talthybius.

(To Servant.)

Please, you were my servant once in days
that though recent now seem years away,
please would you go down to the shore for me,

34

and bring some water here for me to wash
my daughter with, this one last time.
A bride with no wedding deflowered by death
I'll wash her and lay her out as best I can.
She deserves far more. What can I do?
I'll collect things from my fellow captives
who live inside this tent we have to share.
They might have things they've smuggled out of Troy
their lords and masters haven't robbed them of.

Exit Servant.

O splendid palaces! Once happy homes!
O Priam blessed with wealth and all our children
I'm the withered mother of, and none are here.
We've come to nothing, robbed of all regard.
Can any man feel bloated in his pride,
this one of his wealth, and that his name?
They all mean nothing, wishful thinking, boasts,
The happiest human's one who day by day
collides with no misfortune on his way.

Exit Hecuba into the tent.

CHORUS
The whole thing, Troy, our menfolk killed,
our slave fate, worse than being dead,
one man, Paris set in motion,
once he'd felled the pine to build
a ship to sail across the ocean
to fetch back Helen for his bed,
Helen, Helen, the loveliest one
ever shone on by the sun

That set off the cycle. We were caught,
trapped in a conflict we could only lose.
We saw it coming but our limbs felt tied,
fettered before fate's Juggernaut.
Then total havoc. Thousands died.

Because Paris made the fatal choice
and gave Aphrodite beauty's crown
destruction came and dragged Troy down.

Though they've seen their country win,
fate's not spared the women of the Greeks
and mothers on the conqueror's side
mourn like us their sons who've died.
They tear their hair. They gouge their cheeks,
their nails all clogged with gore and skin.

*Enter the Servant followed by the corpse of Polydorus
carried by two women.*

SERVANT
Where's Hecuba? The unluckiest of all.
Hecuba wins the victor's crown for woe
against all comers. No one can compete.

CHORUS
It sounds as though you're bringing bad news too.
Is there no end to messengers of horror?

SERVANT
The bad news is for Hecuba again,
a bitter truth no language can make sweet.

CHORUS
Well, here she is, on cue to hear your news.

Hecuba enters from the central tent.

SERVANT
Your suffering's too great to be expressed,
like a living death still in the light of day.
Children, husband, city, totally wiped out.

HECUBA
That isn't news. Just salt in all my wounds.
But why have you brought my daughter's body here?
I thought the Greeks were keen to dig her grave.

SERVANT
(*aside*)
She's no idea. She's keening for Polyxena
and hasn't grasped that there's another grief.

HECUBA
Not Cassandra? Not Cassandra that you've brought?
Not my little prophetess beneath that sheet?

SERVANT
Cassandra's safe. This man you've never mourned.
I'll lift the sheet and let you see his face.
I fear you're in for the profoundest shock.

HECUBA
My son! My son Polydorus. Dead!
The son that Polymestor was protecting!
I'm destroyed, destroyed. I'm finished off.

My little boy! My little boy!
My whole being wants to wail.
Now with this most recent blow
I see the fiend behind my woe,
the demon always on my trail
the angry demon who'll destroy.

CHORUS
All your fears for him proved true!

HECUBA
Beyond belief, beyond belief,
grief piled on the top of grief.
There'll never be a day
I don't shed tears,
there'll never be a day
I don't heave sighs.
Every day I'll ever know
will have its hours crammed with woe.

CHORUS
We know how you suffer so have we.

HECUBA
Doomed child of a doomed mama
how did you meet your doom,
lying so still, to move no more?
Murdered, murdered, how? by whom?

SERVANT
I don't know. I found him on the shore.

HECUBA
Washed up drowned, or was he stabbed
by a deadly blade on the bare sand?

SERVANT
The waves cast his corpse onto the beach.

HECUBA
That vision that scared me this morning
the phantom with wings like a crow's
now I understand its meaning –
you're lost to the light of Zeus.

CHORUS
Who killed him? Does your dream give you clues?

HECUBA
Our trusted friend, the one it shouldn't be,
who Polydorus was 'protected' by.

CHORUS
No. No. Did he kill him for the gold?

HECUBA
There are no words for it. No name.
Imagination can't conceive such crime.
Utterly unholy, not to be borne.
Hosts and guests are still a sacred bond.
Curse you, curse you, you who hacked

him, hacked. All his limbs are ripped and torn.
Had you no pity for your old friend's son?

CHORUS
Some god with a great grudge let his weight fall
on top of you, the most crushed of us all.

From now on say no more, I see the form
of our master Agamemnon coming here.

Enter Agamemnon.

AGAMEMNON
Why do you delay your daughter's burial?
Talthybius relayed us your request
that no Greek soldiers should lay hands on her.
That's been respected. No one's touched your child.
So I'm surprised you're taking so much time.
I've come to fetch you. Everything back there's
been done properly, if properly's
a word that can be used for things like this.
That corpse though by the tent? Whose body's that?
Must be a Trojan's as his clothes aren't Greek.

HECUBA
(*aside*)
Hecuba! Tell me what I should do.
Throw myself at Agamemnon's feet
Or suffer and not say a single word?

AGAMEMNON
Why do you turn your back on me and cry
and don't say what's been done? Who *is* that man?

HECUBA
(*aside*)
But if he pushes me away from him
wanting no foe or slave to clasp his knees
I'll only bring more suffering on myself.

39

AGAMEMNON
I'm not a mind-reader, which means I can't
know your thoughts unless you tell me them.

HECUBA
(*aside*)
Am I making him more hostile than he is?

AGAMEMNON
If you want to keep me in the dark, that's fine.
I'm honestly not sure I want to know.

HECUBA
(*aside*)
Without his help I can't avenge my child.
Hecuba, don't keep on vacillating. Act!
Just have the bravery, succeed or not.

HECUBA
(*to Agamemnon*)
I beseech you, Agamemnon, by your knees,
your beard, and your conqueror's right hand.

AGAMEMNON
What favour do you want? Is it your freedom?
Your freedom's granted easily enough.

HECUBA
No, never! To get revenge on criminals
I'd live the rest of life out as a slave.

AGAMEMNON
So what's the kind of help you're asking for?

HECUBA
For something you don't know about, my lord.
You see the corpse for whom I make these moans?

AGAMEMNON
Yes, but not much wiser what it means.

HECUBA

I carried him. I gave him birth. He's mine.

AGAMEMNON

One of yours, poor woman, but which one?

HECUBA

Not one of Priam's sons who died in war.

AGAMEMNON

Besides those there was this one that you bore?

HECUBA

To not much purpose. He's the one you see.

AGAMEMNON

When Troy was being sacked then where was he?

HECUBA

His father packed him off, afraid he'd die.

AGAMEMNON

This son he picked where was he packed off to?

HECUBA

Here, where his corpse has just been found.

AGAMEMNON

To Polymestor, ruler of this land?

HECUBA

Yes, sent with Trojan gold that sealed his doom.

AGAMEMNON

How did he meet his downfall? And by whom?

HECUBA

It was by his Thracian host that he was killed.

AGAMEMNON

Savage! He did the deed through lust for gold?

HECUBA

Yes, once he knew that Troy had met its end.

AGAMEMNON

Who brought the body here? Where was he found?

HECUBA

This woman came across him on the beach.

AGAMEMNON

Doing other things or did she search?

HECUBA

Fetching water from the sea to wash my child.

AGAMEMNON

He flung him in the sea once he'd been killed?

HECUBA

Pummelled in the spume, his body slashed to pieces.

AGAMEMNON

Poor woman, it seems your suffering never ceases.

HECUBA

I'm finished, Agamemnon. There can't be more in store.

AGAMEMNON

Ahh! Ahh! What woman has borne more?

HECUBA

Let me tell you why I grasp your knees.
If you believe my suffering's ordained
I'll say no more, but if you don't think that
help me take vengeance on that evil man
who broke every bond of friendship by his deed,
fearing neither gods below nor gods above.
Though I may be both a slave and powerless,
even the lowly are allowed the law.
Our beliefs, our codes are all a search for law,
our only way of knowing right from wrong.

If you allow the law to be corrupted
and nothing's done to punish those who kill
their guests, and violate the holy places,
there's no safe centre in the lives of men.
So count these crimes as shameful. Show regard
for me and stand back like a painter does
and notice the detail of the pains endured.
Once I was a queen. Now I'm your slave.
Once blessed with children. Now I'm old with none.
I have no city. Sunk in desolation
the bleakest and most abject of mankind.

Pathetic wretch! I won't achieve a thing!
You're creeping off! You're making your escape.
Is my misery too much to comprehend?

Why do we mortals waste time in acquiring
knowledge of various kinds, but when it comes
to persuasion, we can't spare the fees
to learn as thoroughly as time permits
the only art on which all power depends
so with eloquence's magic we'd give words
to what we want and words would help us win.
So why am I still hoping for success?
The sons I had aren't living any more.
I'm a captive in debasing servitude.
I see the smoke-clouds glowering over Troy.

Though you may think that this is out of place
to bring in passion as a plea, I will.
What are they worth to you, those nights of love?
What will Cassandra get for those embraces
so lovingly given in your mutual bed?
And what benefit will I her mother get?

Listen! You see that dead man over there?
Help him. You have a bond of kinship now.

I'm not making any headway with my plea.

43

I wish I had voices in my arms and lips,
in my fingertips, my hair, and both my feet
contrived by Daedalus or by some god
so my entire choir could grasp your knees
and all my many voices make their pleas.
Master, the shining beacon of the Greeks,
help an old woman get her retribution.
Maybe she's nothing. Do it nonetheless.
A good man commits himself to justice
and combats the wicked in whatever place.

CHORUS

Compulsion can take all our choice away.
Sometimes we're forced to make old foes our friends
and the best of friends the bitterest of foes.

AGAMEMNON

I pity you, your son, what you've both suffered,
and I'm sympathetic to your suppliant's appeal.
I hope, for the sake of justice and the gods,
you get due reckoning from your treacherous friend.
I hope, that's if it could be brought about
so it both went well for you, and I'd avoid
the men believing that I'd plot to kill
the Thracian king to gratify Cassandra.

There's one more thing I've got to bear in mind.
The men count Polymestor as a friend
and your dead son, being Trojan, as a foe.
If I count Polydorus as my friend
that's my affair, that matters just to me,
but it's not a feeling that the army shares.
Bear this in mind. I'd gladly help, you know,
and share your load and rush to your defence,
but not if it means censure from the Greeks.

HECUBA

Show me a mortal man who's really free.
He's either a slave to money or to chance.

Or the pressure of the mob or legal code
curbs him from acting as his will dictates.
If you quail before the common herd
and give it too much weight, I'll set you free.
Share in the knowledge of my plot against
the murderer, but don't share in the deed.
If the army's in an uproar and they aid
the Thracian when he gets what he deserves
use your authority to hold them back
but not so they know you're doing it for me.

As for the rest, don't worry. I'll take care of that.

AGAMEMNON

You? How? Will you take a sword in your old hand
and kill the barbarian yourself, or poison him?
Who'll help you? Where do you have friends?

HECUBA

There are a lot of Trojan women in that tent.

AGAMEMNON

You mean the slaves, the spear-spoil of the Greeks?

HECUBA

They'll help me to avenge my slaughtered son.

AGAMEMNON

How can you women overpower a man?

HECUBA

Enough of them would scare you soon enough
and with cunning they're a force hard to resist.

AGAMEMNON

Scary, perhaps. But, on the strength scale, short.

HECUBA

History's full of tales of bands of women
overpowering men: like the Danaids,
or Lemnos completely cleansed of all its men . . .

Enough of that. Let's not pursue the theme.
Give this woman a safe conduct through the ranks.

(*To Servant.*)
Approach King Polymestor, and say this:
Hecuba, once Queen of Troy, requests you come
as much for your own benefit as hers.
And for your sons' benefit. They too should know
what Hecuba has to tell you and tell them.

Exit Servant.

(*To Agamemnon.*)
Agamemnon, please delay the funeral rites
for Polyxena who's just been put to death,
so brother and sister, my double grief,
can burn on the same pyre and share one tomb.

AGAMEMNON

I'll see to it. If the army could set sail
there'd be no way this favour could be granted.
But as it is the army has to wait
in enforced idleness to put to sea.
The gods won't send one breath of favouring breeze.
We kick our heels and hope the wind comes soon.
Somehow I hope it turns out for the best.
I think the wish is common among men,
as individuals and citizens,
that bad men should suffer and good men thrive.

Exit Agamemnon.

CHORUS

Troy, Troy, my fatherland,
till Greece invaded never sacked,
your towers now no longer stand.
The choking mass of Greeks attacked,
spear after spear, the massive thrust,
Those towers that were once your crown
were shattered and came crashing down

all their glory smoke and dust.
My fate forbids me to set foot
ever again, where flame and soot
have branded and defiled our town.

It was midnight when my doom began
when a delicious drowsiness descends.
Because we knew the Greeks had gone
we'd celebrated with our friends.
In gratitude for our relief
my husband made a sacrifice
and lay in bed and breathed in peace
thankful we were still alive.
The first night he'd hung up his spear
and gone to bed without the fear
of the invading force of Greece.

I was putting my hair up in a braid
daydreaming at the endless deep
of the mirror, where gold lights shone bright,
preparing myself for love and sleep,
when shouting and shrill screaming
shattered my boudoir daydreaming.
Greeks! Everywhere you heard them scream
you heard the savage yells and whoops
of slaughter-glutted, sex-starved troops:
'Let's finish it off and fuck off home.'

I had only my shift on when I fled
to the shrine of Artemis where I thought
I'd be safer than in our marriage bed
but hugging her statue went for nought.
I had to watch my husband hacked
to bloody pieces. Me, they dragged
off to the ships and away to sea.
I see Troy recede and know its streets
are blackened rubble, craters, weeds,
and grief, huge grief floods over me.

I sent my cry across the brine
cursing Helen for the loss
of everything I'd loved as mine,
husband, city, gutted house.
And I cursed Paris, he who wed,
(if wedding it can be called)
the demon who heaped up thousands dead,
sons, husbands, fathers, brothers killed.
May she feel the sickening wrench
of leaving home and never returning,
of longing for a home she'll never see.
I pray as a small revenge
for all our dead and for Troy's burning
Helen ends up a refugee.

Enter Polymestor and Guards.

POLYMESTOR

Hecuba, I weep to see your city over there
still smoking, you in such a state, the body
here of Polyxena who's just been killed.
Aaahhh
Nothing can be trusted, city and good name
or that a man's good luck can't turn out bad.
The gods stir life together back and forth
adding confusion to the mix so we'll revere
the gods out of uncertainty at what comes next.

Keening can't clear the undergrowth of grief.

If you're about to blame me for my absence,
wait! I was away in the interior of Thrace
when you came here. As soon as I got back
your woman met me at the very moment
I was setting off to see you from my house.
As soon as I heard her message then I came.

HECUBA

I'm ashamed to look you in the face

HECUBA

now I find myself in such a dreadful plight.
In front of one who's seen me in my glory
I'm ashamed you find me in this abject state.
I daren't look you in the eye, though that implies
no ill-will towards you, and no offence.

POLYMESTOR

And no offence is taken. What can I do?
Why did you send for me to come from home?

HECUBA

Something private you, and your sons, should know.
Ask your attendants to stand further back.

POLYMESTOR

Leave! I need no protection here. It's safe.
You are my friend. The Greek troops are my friends.
Tell me, what service can I render you?
How can one who flourishes help friends in need?
I'll willingly do everything I can.

HECUBA

First tell me of my son, Polydorus.
His father and I entrusted to your care.
Other questions later. First things first.
Is my son Polydorus still alive?

POLYMESTOR

He is! With him at least your luck's still in.

HECUBA

My dear friend, what good news! All thanks to you!

POLYMESTOR

The other questions? What do you want to know?

HECUBA

Is his old mother ever in his thoughts?

POLYMESTOR

He wanted to come and give you a surprise.

49

HECUBA
The gold he brought from Troy? Is that still safe?

POLYMESTOR
Safe under lock and key back at my house.

HECUBA
Keep it safe! No coveting what's not yours!

POLYMESTOR
Goes without saying. My own gold does for me.

HECUBA
Do you know what I need to tell you and your sons?

POLYMESTOR
No idea! You'll let me know in your own words.

HECUBA
There are . . . dear friend as much now as before . . .

POLYMESTOR
What is it that my sons and I should know?

HECUBA
. . . hidden caves with the gold of Priam's sons.

POLYMESTOR
Is this something that you want your son to know?

HECUBA
Yes, through you. You're someone I can trust.

POLYMESTOR
But why do we need the presence of my sons?

HECUBA
It's better they know too, in case you die.

POLYMESTOR
You're right, of course. Your plan shows some
forethought.

HECUBA
You know Athena's cave-shrine back in Troy.

POLYMESTOR
The gold's there, is it? Is it marked at all?

HECUBA
An outcrop of black rock juts from the earth.

POLYMESTOR
Do you want to tell me more about what's there?

HECUBA
I'd like you to guard the money I've brought out.

POLYMESTOR
Where is it? Is it hidden in your clothes?

HECUBA
Safe in the tent with other precious things.

POLYMESTOR
But it's close to where the Greeks have moored their ships.

HECUBA
The captive women's tents are out of bounds.

POLYMESTOR
So it's all safe inside? No men about?

HECUBA
Not one! Only us women on our own.
Come in and see our home. The Greeks can't wait
to get on board and set sail home from Troy.
Come in, get what it's only right you get,
then go back with your boys, go back to where
you've given shelter to my son and heir.

Polymestor follows Hecuba into the tent.

CHORUS
You haven't yet paid for your crime
but now, but now, it's time, it's time.

Like a man alone on the ocean wave
not a haven or harbour in sight
suddenly lurched out of his life
pitched over his life's side.

You haven't yet paid for your crime
but now, but now, it's time, it's time.

When the gods call in their debt
and Justice wants your scalp as well,
better for you if you were dead
as your life will be one long hell.

You haven't yet paid for your crime
but now, but now, it's time, it's time.

If your hopes were high, you were conned.
The road ends in Hades' cul-de-sac
and you quit life slain by a hand
never trained to slash and hack.

You haven't yet paid for your crime
but *now*, it's time, it's time, it's time.

POLYMESTOR
Aggghh! Agghhh! My eyes! Blinded! Blinded! Dark! Dark!

CHORUS
Listen to the Thracian screaming, friends.

POLYMESTOR
My sons! My sons! They've butchered both of them!

CHORUS
Dreadful things are done inside the tent.

POLYMESTOR
You can't escape! However fast you flee!
I'll tear this tent to little shreds and tatters.

CHORUS
Shall we burst in? Now it's time we stood
alongside Hecuba and all the others.

HECUBA

Enter Hecuba from the tent.

HECUBA

Tear away, spare nothing. Tear the whole tent down.
You'll never get the light back in your eyes
and even with your eyes you'll never see
your sons alive again. I've murdered them!

CHORUS

Did you really overpower your Thracian friend?
And did you do those things you said you did?

HECUBA

You'll see him coming now out from the tent,
blind, and bungling about with blind man's steps.
You'll see the bodies of his sons I did to death
helped by that brave band of Trojan women.
I've got my justice and he's paid the price.
Look, he's coming now out of the tent.
I'll keep back though. Volcanic Thracian wrath,
there's no contending with it once unleashed.

POLYMESTOR

Where go? Where stop? Where's safe?
On all fours like a mountain beast
sniffing the trail. Which way?
That? This?
I want to get my claws into them,
these terrorists from Troy
who've destroyed me.
Savage, savage women,
Curse you with a thousand curses.
Where've they escaped to?
Where are they cowering?
Where've they fled to?
Heal! Heal my sight, Helios,
Sun put light back
in my blood-blinded eyes!

Aaaggh! aaaggh!

Sssh! I can sense them
the women tiptoeing about.
How can I leap on them
gorge blood, crunch bone,
a beast's blood-glut.
Revenge! Revenge!
outrage for outrage,
mangling for mangling.

Now where am I off to?
Abandoning my children
to the mercy of these maniacs,
maenads, berserk bacchantes,
tearing their bodies apart,
butchered, dismembered,
a blood-dunked banquet
slung out on the crags for the dogs.

Where stop? Turn? Go?

My billowing robe
a wind-blown sail
tugging its rigging
speeding to protect
my sons' cold corpses
from the maws of monsters,
wild beasts in their lair.

CHORUS
Your suffering's extreme and terrible to bear
but no more than your vicious act deserves.

POLYMESTOR
Ai ai!
Thracians help me,
my spearmen, my soldiers,
my warrior horsemen.

Greeks, sons of Atreus,

can't you hear me shouting?
Help! Help! Help!
For the gods' sake, hurry.
Over here! Over here!
Does nobody hear me?
Will nobody help me?
What are you waiting for?
The women have destroyed me,
your captive slaves.
My pain's unbearable.
Violation! Outrage!
Where can I turn to? Where go?
Fly up to the heavens
where the hunter Orion
and Sirius his dog
dart beams of fire
out of their eyes?
Or sail a black ferry
off to Hades in grief?

CHORUS

A man who's suffered more than enough
can be forgiven if he wants to quit life.

Enter Agamemnon.

AGAMEMNON

I came when I heard the screaming. Hardly quiet
the echo off the crags that scared the troops.
If we didn't know we'd razed Troy to the ground
the Greeks would be panicked by this sudden din.

POLYMESTOR

Agamemnon, my dearest friend, I knew
as soon as I heard your voice that it was you.
Look at the violence that's been done to me.

AGAMEMNON

Ah!

Polymestor, poor wretch. Who's brought you down?
Who's mashed your blinded eyeballs into pulp?
Who killed these boys? Whoever did the deed
nursed a huge grudge against you and your sons.

POLYMESTOR
Hecuba! The women prisoners. It was them.
They destroyed me, no, far more than destroyed.

AGAMEMNON
What are you saying?

(*To Hecuba.*)
Did you do the deed,
Hecuba? How did you find such nerves of steel?

POLYMESTOR
What's that? Is that bitch Hecuba hereabouts?
Show me! Show me where she is, so I can get
my claws into her flesh and rip her body
into bits of carcass and a flood of blood.

AGAMEMNON
You can't do that!

POLYMESTOR
I beg you by the gods
let me just get my wild hands on the bitch.

AGAMEMNON
Don't act like a savage. Calm your soul.
Tell me your tale. I'll hear you both in turn
and try to judge why you have suffered this.

POLYMESTOR
I'll tell you the whole tale. The youngest son
of Hecuba and Priam was sent from Troy
by his father, who feared that Troy would fall,
to be under my protection in my house.
I had him put to death. I'll tell you why,

and why it showed good thinking, good forethought.
I feared the boy as a surviving foe
might refound the city and remobilise.
And once they knew that one of Priam's sons
was still alive the Greeks would have to mount
another expedition against Troy,
and plunder the plains of Thrace for provender.
Those of us living next to Troy would suffer
the sort of things we've recently gone through.

When Hecuba found out about her son
she lured me here by spinning me some yarn
of chests of royal gold concealed at Troy.
She coaxed me and my sons inside the tent
under the pretext no one else should know.
I sat down on a bed, relaxed, at ease.
The women, on my right and on my left,
sat close to me as they'd sit close to friends
and admired the embroidered handiwork
and the weaving of the clothing that I wore.
They held my cloak against the light to see
the closeness of the famed Edonian weave.
Others admired my pair of Thracian spears
and before I realised I'd been disarmed.
Those who'd been mothers cooed at my two boys
and jigged them on their knees and passed them round
so that I'd be at some distance from my sons.

Then suddenly the tender chatter changed
and, all at once, they pulled blades from their robes
and stabbed my boys, while others grabbed my arms
and legs, and, like octopuses, held me down.
I wanted to save my boys but every time
I tried to raise my head they gripped my hair.
I'd try to move my hands. I couldn't stir.
They crowded round to make sure I kept still.
Then, finally, a pain beyond all pain,

57

they wreaked their worst on me. My eyes. My eyes.
They grabbed their cloak-clasps and they burst my eyes,
stabbing both pupils to a bloody pulp.
Then they were off in full flight from the tent.
I leaped like a wild beast in pursuit
of the abominable bitches round the tent
lunging and flailing like a beast gone frantic.

I've suffered this for furthering your cause
and killing your enemy, Agamemnon.
Not to go on too long, if any man
in the past, the present or the future said
bad things about women, let me top them all
and say: sea or land breeds nothing worse.
Even a brief encounter proves it true.

CHORUS
Don't take that insolent abusive tone!
Your suffering doesn't write off all our sex.

HECUBA
Agamemnon, men shouldn't believe a speech
counts for far more than actions ever did.
If a man is good in deed, he's good in word.
But bad deeds make a man's word rotten too,
and he can't give his injustice a fair gloss.
They're clever with their tongues so finely tuned
but you couldn't call them clever in the end.
Their punishment will come. No one escapes.

That's by way of a preamble to my speech.
Now I'll turn to him and make my counter-plea.
You killed my son for Agamemnon's sake
and to spare the Greeks a second Trojan War,
or so you claim, you criminal. Not so!
First, consider barbarians and Greeks.
They're never likely, ever, to be friends.
Greeks don't make friends of backward brutes like you.

What was behind that zealousness of yours?
A marriage alliance? Kinship connection?
What were you after? Were the Greeks once more
on their way back to lay your country waste?
And who, I ask you, 's taken in by that?
If you could tell the truth your motive's gold.
Gold killed my son. Gold. Your greed for gold.
Explain me this: how was it that when Troy
and her encircling battlements still stood,
and Priam lived, and Hector won all bouts,
how was it, if you wanted to impress the Greeks,
you didn't kill the boy right there and then
while you were raising him in your own house
or bring him to the Argives still alive?
But once the Trojans had been finished off
and smoke sent signals foes had taken Troy
that's when you chose to murder your child guest.
And another thing to show how vile you are,
if you'd wanted to promote the Argive cause,
the gold which wasn't yours but my dead son's
you should have made a gift of to the Greeks
who were in need and desperate for funds,
so long away and so cut off from Greece.
You still can't let the gold out of your grasp,
and still persist in hoarding it at home.
If you'd brought my boy up and protected him
as you were duty bound and should have done
you would have earned an honourable name.
Friends shine out most clearly in bad times.
When things are good then everyone's your friend.
If you'd been short of funds, then once my son
had come into his own, he'd share his wealth.
But as it is you can't count him a friend.
What good you might have got out of the gold
is, like your joy in your two children, gone.
And you, you're in the state you're in.

Agamemnon,

this is what I'd like to say to you.
Helping him will make you look as base.
You'd be doing good to one who as a host
broke all restraints of reverence and trust.
We'll say that you take pleasure in vile men
because you're like that too. But look at me,
a slave saying such things to her master's face.

CHORUS
Good words always start out from good deeds.

AGAMEMNON
(aside)
Crime involving others is for me
burdensome to judge. And yet I must.
I said I'd deal with this and must persist.
If I abandon it, it brings me shame.

(To Polymestor.)
If you want to know what I think, I think this.
You killed your guest, but not on my behalf,
or the coalition's, but to confiscate his gold.
Now things have gone against you, you just say
anything at all to plead your cause.
Perhaps for lesser breeds it's no great thing
to kill a guest, but to us Greeks it is.
If I say you did no wrong I can't escape
the censure and the blame that I'll incur.
Since you were tough enough to do such deeds
be tough enough to suffer the results.

POLYMESTOR
Aaaggh! Worsted by a woman and a slave!
I undergo an underdog's revenge.

HECUBA
Isn't that just? Your crimes were hideous.

POLYMESTOR
But the pain I'm in. My children! And my eyes!

HECUBA
You feel pain as I do for my son.

POLYMESTOR
You love insulting me, you cruel bitch!

HECUBA
Why shouldn't I enjoy my sweet revenge?

POLYMESTOR
You won't enjoy it once the ocean wave . . .

HECUBA
. . . carries me to slavery in Greece?

POLYMESTOR
No! covers you when you fall off the mast.

HECUBA
Who'll force me to leap off from such a height?

POLYMESTOR
You'll shin up the ship's mast all by yourself.

HECUBA
How, unless I grew wings on my back?

POLYMESTOR
You'll turn into a bitch with blazing eyes.

HECUBA
How do you know about my change of shape?

POLYMESTOR
Through Dionysus, prophet/god of Thrace.

HECUBA
Pity your prophet didn't prophesy your pain.

POLYMESTOR
If he had would I have fallen for your trick?

HECUBA
Does the prophet say I'll die here or survive?

POLYMESTOR
Die! And where you'll be buried will be called . . .

HECUBA
. . . not some name referring to my shape!

POLYMESTOR
The Bitch's Grave, a headland sailors shun.

HECUBA
Now you've been made to pay, why should I care?

POLYMESTOR
Your daughter Cassandra, she'll die too.

HECUBA
Those evil words I spit back in your face.

POLYMESTOR
She'll be killed by Agamemnon's bitter spouse.

HECUBA
His Clytemnestra can't go mad that way.

POLYMESTOR
She'll kill him with her. Wielding a great axe.

AGAMEMNON
Are you insane? Or wanting to be flogged?

POLYMESTOR
Go ahead. Kill me if you want. A bath,
a bloody bath in Argos waits for you!

AGAMEMNON
Guards, drag this man away out of my sight!

POLYMESTOR
Can't you bear to hear?

AGAMEMNON
Stop his drivelling mouth!

POLYMESTOR
Gag me. All's said anyway.

AGAMEMNON
Ship him off!
Find a desert island, some bleak rock
where beasts like him may howl and not be heard.

Guards remove Polymestor.

AGAMEMNON
Hecuba, quickly, bury both your dead
and you, women of Troy, must now collect
at your masters' tents. I feel the winds
have come to waft our vessels swiftly home.
May all our ships fare well.
Now free from war
I pray we find our happiness back home.

CHORUS
Go to the shoreline and our masters' tents.
Find out from them what work we're forced to do.
We've got no choice. No choice at all. We're slaves.

The End.

FRAM

Acknowledgements

Grateful thanks are due as ever to Marion Holland for invaluable help with research, and to those actors who did a week's *Fram* workshop at the National Theatre Studio in 2006: David Bradley, Max Dowler, Michael Feast, Caroline Gruber, Tanya Moodie, Colin Stinton, Sian Thomas, Joseph Thompson and Peter Wight; and to Ann Morrish and Sian Thomas, who read extracts of *Fram* with me at the European Cultural Centre of Delphi, Greece, in 2006.

Tony Harrison
March 2008

Fram was first presented in the Olivier auditorium of the National Theatre, London, on 10 April 2008. The cast was as follows:

Gilbert Murray Jeff Rawle
Sybil Thorndike Sian Thomas
Fridtjof Nansen Jasper Britton
Hjalmar Johansen Mark Addy
Ballerina Viviana Durante
ARA Men
  Stuart Shaw Jim Creighton
  James Callaghan Steven Helliwell
  William H. Rutland Joseph Thompson
  Sheldon, ARA Chief (Moscow) Patrick Drury
Eglantyne Jebb Carolyn Pickles
Ruth Fry Clare Lawrence
Kurdish Poet Aykut Hilmi
Stowaways Ronald Chabvuka, Joel Davis,
  Verelle Roberts, Keanu Taylor

Directors Tony Harrison and Bob Crowley
Set Designer Bob Crowley
Costume Designer Fotini Dimou
Lighting Designer Mark Henderson
Music Richard Blackford
Video Designer Jon Driscoll
Choreographer Wayne McGregor
Sound Designer Gareth Fry
Production Manager Diane Willmott
Staff Director Max Key
Stage Manager Maggie Tully
Deputy Stage Manager Janice Heyes
Assistant Stage Managers Peter Gregory, Julia Wickham

Characters

Gilbert Murray

Sybil Thorndike

Fridtjof Nansen

Hjalmar Johansen

Ballerina

ARA Men

Sheldon

Eglantyne Jebb

Ruth Fry

Kurdish Poet

Stowaways

Part One

Westminster Abbey. The sound of late organ practice
echoes in the empty Abbey. Then the organist stops,
shuts off the organ, turns off the lights and we hear his
echoing footsteps reverberating in the Abbey and the
opening creak and echoing closing slam of a huge
wooden door.

Poets' Corner and across the way the memorial to
Gilbert Murray.

A cloud moves away from the full moon and its light
streams through the Rose Window, and sheds the image
of Aeschylus into the air like an Aurora. Then it falls on
the memorial plaque to Gilbert Murray.

Gilbert Murray emerges after fifty years beneath his
plaque.

He stands in the coloured light cast by the image of
Aeschylus.

He looks up at the Rose Window and addresses
Aeschylus.

GILBERT MURRAY

Aeschylus? I don't believe it. You! You! it's you
in Westminster Abbey the moon is shining through.
My ecstatic ashes find themselves illuminated
by the spirit of the poet I'm so proud to have translated.
The light's like an Aurora and I rejoice, rejoice
that I was ever chosen to be your English voice.
Aeschylus! Your radiance is like the bright Aurora
described to me by Nansen, my friend, the explorer,
who's the protagonist I've chosen in the fifty years I've
    spent

composing my own drama beneath my monument.
Aeschylus! Aeschylus! O Aeschylus, I knew
the light that woke my spirit could only come from you.
So, greatest of tragedians, I beg you to assist
my humblest of efforts to become a dramatist.
With your inspiration I hope our play succeeds
in honouring Fridtjof Nansen and his heroic deeds,
from the Polar ice floes he sailed his ship the *Fram* in
to his noble role in saving millions from famine.

> *Gilbert Murray sees a fresh green laurel wreath*
> *laid on a plaque in the floor of Poets' Corner,*
> *though he doesn't see that it is laid on the memorial*
> *to T. S. Eliot.*

This drama I'm preparing 'll earn me a laurel wreath
like this one laid to honour the poet who lies beneath.

> *Takes wreath, then looks back at plaque.*

Oh no! Oh no! It beggars all belief.
T. S. Eliot! He's not worth one laurel leaf.
What a tasteless, not to say a crudely crass idea
to place Eliot in this spot when I'm not far from here.
What a dastardly, mean and spiteful trick to play
to put my cruellest critic just seventy feet away!

> *Gilbert Murray walks away from the T. S. Eliot*
> *memorial and tries on the wreath for size.*

This could be the laurel wreath I'll be allowed to wear
once I've shown the Muses my true poetic flair.
And once I've got the crown on I'll be finally allowed
to cross the floor to mingle with the Poets' Corner crowd.
Me in Poets' Corner! My deepest dream come true!
Provided they don't put me next to you-know-who!

> *Gilbert Murray begins to walk towards Poets' Corner*
> *to replace the laurel wreath, then decides to keep it*

*and place it on his own memorial. He contemplates
the wreath on his carved name.*

I know! I need Sybil Thorndike, my Hecuba, Medea.
Her ashes, I believe, are also resting here.

*Gilbert Murray begins to walk through the Abbey
searching for Sybil Thorndike.*

Sybil! It's Gilbert! I've been let out on parole.
I'm going to do a drama and want you to play a role.
Sybil! Sybil!

SYBIL THORNDIKE
Gilbert! No need to go so far.
I'm just round the corner from where your ashes are.
Right here next to Noël, who died in 1973.
I played Lady Gilpin in his *Hands Across the Sea*,
the same year I played Aphrodite and the Nurse
in your *Hippolytus*. I'm happiest with verse.
And your verse, whatever critics say, I find divine.
I went on playing your Medea till I was fifty-nine!

GILBERT MURRAY
I know that very well, that's why I wanted you.
There's a part in this drama I rather hope you'll do.

SYBIL THORNDIKE
What as?

GILBERT MURRAY
As yourself, dear Sybil.

SYBIL THORNDIKE
As myself, oh dear!
I get stage fright as myself.

GILBERT MURRAY
Please say that you'll appear.

SYBIL THORNDIKE

What's it about? Is it one of your translations?

GILBERT MURRAY

No, Sybil, an original, and my inspiration 's
Dr Fridtjof Nansen. I call my drama FRAM.

SYBIL THORNDIKE

Fram? Sounds like Beckett! Beckett SAM
not the Thomas à Becket of T. S. El—

GILBERT MURRAY

That name's taboo.

SYBIL THORNDIKE

Sorry, darling! Yes, he made cruel fun of you.

GILBERT MURRAY

T. S. Eliot! Who damned my versions of Greek plays,
saying they were ruined by my 'Swinburnian haze'.
'With no creative instinct he leaves Euripides quite dead'
is what you-know-who (that dreadful playwright!) said.
And would you believe it, the Abbey powers-that-be
have put his memorial only seventy feet from me!

SYBIL THORNDIKE

Surely, Gilbert Murray, this slightly petty streak
is scarcely compatible with chairs in ancient Greek!
Before I mentioned you-know-who and made you so upset
you said your play was called . . . what was it? I forget.

GILBERT MURRAY

FRAM ('FORWARD' in Norwegian), what Nansen called
the craft
he had specially constructed with round hull fore and aft,
so that, when the pack-ice crushed it, it didn't crack, but
rose
and stayed unshattered on top of the ice floes.
So with my modest talents as the would-be poet I am

that is my subject – Fridtjof Nansen and the *Fram*.
Fram, and famine, is the play I hope to write.

SYBIL THORNDIKE
Hope to write, Gilbert? When's it for?

GILBERT MURRAY
Tonight!

SYBIL THORNDIKE
Tonight? Tonight? But where's my part? We haven't time.

GILBERT MURRAY
But we're already talking in Gilbert Murray rhyme!
All you have to do is remember who you've been
and you'll be absolutely capable of playing any scene.

SYBIL THORNDIKE
Which theatre will have the honour of me playing me?

GILBERT MURRAY
The National Theatre, Sybil, on the South Bank, the 'NT'!
And, Sybil, you'll be thrilled to know that you will play
in the space named for your friend, Lord Olivier
(who resides near Poets' Corner, by the way).

SYBIL THORNDIKE
(*shouting*)

Larry?

GILBERT MURRAY
Not so loud! He'll hear you, and immediately start
demanding that he gets the drama's leading part.

SYBIL THORNDIKE
He'd be rather good as Nansen.

GILBERT MURRAY
No, Sybil, no,
it's only the originals I'm using in my show.

Nansen's Nansen. Gilbert Murray's me, and you, you're
you.
Everything is real and everything is true.
I think it's time we quietly creep off to the NT
before all the ghosts of thespians start yearning to be free.

SYBIL THORNDIKE
Nansen was so handsome, I remember, like a Viking
when he came to London. To a lot of ladies' liking.
Will he be there?

GILBERT MURRAY
He will.

SYBIL THORNDIKE
Goody! But wish you'd said.
If I'd known I was meeting Nansen I'd've worn my red!

GILBERT MURRAY
You'll be fine just as you are!
Right! Across the river!
You'll appear after the Prologue I myself deliver.

*Gilbert Murray takes a marble mask from a poetic
memorial.
He takes Sybil Thorndike by the hand.
They hurry to the National Theatre. They go
through the foyers to the door into the Olivier stalls.
They enter through the door to the Olivier stalls.*

SYBIL THORNDIKE
(*entering Olivier stalls through right aisle*)
Gilbert! This is so inspiring! The Olivier!
I can't wait to walk onto that stage and do your play.

GILBERT MURRAY
(*entering Olivier stalls through left aisle*)
Just imagine, Sybil, this space we see before us
was inspired by the theatre of ancient Epidaurus.

But the balcony's scarcely authentic ancient Greek.
Remember someone's up there, though, every time you
  speak.

SYBIL THORNDIKE

Gilbert you're addressing one who was renowned
throughout her lifetime for her clarity of sound.
Everything I utter will be crystal clear.
Even those in ten-quid seats have a right to hear.

Sybil Thorndike moves closer to the stage, then stops.

Gilbert, you resurrect me, give me no time to prepare,
let me come in the wrong frock and with frightful hair.
You should have given me time to choose another dress,
something less tomb-bound. Look, my hair's a total mess.

*Sybil Thorndike and Gilbert Murray go onto the
totally bare Olivier stage and savour its proportions.*

So you haven't got a text? And I see you haven't yet
gone to the trouble to think about a set!
I need costume and make-up, I don't want to disgrace
the memory of my noble friend whose spirit fills this space.
I need to change my costume. I need to do my face!

Sybil Thorndike exits.

GILBERT MURRAY

And while you are doing that I'm going to cover mine
to initiate our effort with one ancient tragic line.

*Gilbert Murray enters with the mask of Greek
Tragedy. He holds it before his face.*

Ουκ αν τις ειποι μαλλον η πεπονθαμεν.   (Eur. *Herc,* 916)

*Revealing himself, and placing mask downstage
centre.*

Not to cast aspersions on your state of education,

but is anyone out there in need of a translation?
Let me see a show of hands. O, I see, quite a lot.
No fellow classicists? Obviously not!
Ουκ αν τις ειποι μαλλον η πεπονθαμεν (*Herakles*),
one of the greatest tragedies of the great Euripides.
The messenger enters. His first words in Greek are these:
Ουκ αν τις ειποι μαλλον η πεπονθαμεν.
What he's saying 's that the horror that's occurred 's
too terrible for anyone to put into mere words.
And then from line nine-two-two to ten-fifteen
he lets us know in detail the horrors that he's seen.
Ninety-three lines in graphic, passionate succession
giving the unspeakable poetical expression.
Forgive the ancient Greek. I'm only showing off.

He bows.

Gilbert Murray, classicist, translator, prof.
As the ghost of Gilbert Murray I've not had to travel far,
just from Westminster Abbey where now my ashes are.
They've been there fifty years exactly. Hence this brief
    parole
and anniversary outing for my long-departed soul,
suddenly awakened by a streaming radiant light
that inspired me to rise and visit you tonight.
I'd hazard a surmise most of you are unaware
there's a stained-glass Aeschylus in the Abbey over there.
I was his translator. There's no poetic fire
blazes brighter in the firmament than his *Oresteia*.
His *Oresteia* was played here, and my question's why,
when my own was in existence, was the version by . . .
(permit me, I beg you, my peck of peevish pique)
a grubby Yorkshire poet with a bad degree in Greek!

Gilbert Murray composes himself.

I'm here as one who had the honour to know between
    the wars

one of the greatest heroes of the international cause,
my friend, Fridtjof Nansen, who died nine years before
our precious League of Nations broke up with the war.
Nansen was a hero who served the League of Nations
starting with his prisoner-of-war repatriations,
then giving the stateless person and the refugee
a means of crossing borders, an ID,
that allowed, for example, many a Russian émigré,
Stravinsky, Chagall, Pavlova, world-renowned today,
to use the special passport that bore his name,
the Nansen passport, to cross frontiers, and find fame.
Now Time's bestowed a Nansen passport on my ghost
to re-enter life and cross extinction's border post
to tell you I, like Nansen, a passionate believer
in the principles of peace we worked for in Geneva,
had to witness the League's failure, and, unlike Nansen,
    then
lived to hope for better from the newly named UN.
Nansen died. I lived, and to my profoundest shame
saw the atrocities enacted in humanity's soiled name.
To speak of the war's atrocities is an almost hopeless task
even for this open-eyed and eloquent Greek mask.
I happen to believe that the ancient tragic speech
is the highest form of eloquence a man can hope to
    reach.

*Sybil Thorndike in a dressing gown over a green dress
shouts from wings.*

SYBIL THORNDIKE

Gilbert!

GILBERT MURRAY

Sybil?

SYBIL THORNDIKE
Is it time for me yet?

GILBERT MURRAY
                            Not yet, no!
Your scene comes after Nansen's scenes in Arctic ice and
    snow.

SYBIL THORNDIKE
Scene? Scene! I can't believe you'd be so mean
to bring me back from oblivion to play one paltry scene!
How cruel to disturb a long-departed soul
only to offer her a less than leading role,
and make her wait while Nansen tries to reach the Pole.
Well, I hope his Arctic *scenes* take Dr Nansen ages.
It will give you time to write me several more pages.
I warn you if my part 's not a satisfactory size
I might have to steal the limelight and simply improvise.
And Gilbert, this costume, I fear that it won't do!
I never appear in costumes in either green or blue!
I can't go on, I warn you, dressed the way I am.
Find me another frock or you can fuck your *Fram*.

GILBERT MURRAY
Language, Sybil, language! I fear that you abuse
the purer vocabulary of my more genteel Muse.

SYBIL THORNDIKE
Well, Gilbert, I hope she won't prove so genteel
she won't do justice to the way that people feel.

GILBERT MURRAY
There are moments, I confess, when she rather shies away
from certain aspects of the subject that I've chosen for
    my play.
Though I admire Nansen with an almost schoolboy awe
I can't cope with the fact he's a fervent carnivore.
As a lifetime vegetarian I find that I can't bear
to describe what was for Nansen his daily Arctic fare.
The bear-brains breakfast fried in blubber of skinned seal
is not what I'd consider a tolerable meal.

And as a teetotaller too my non-imbibing Muse
is somewhat prim and squeamish about Johansen's 'booze'.
Nansen's companion. Johansen, who can only think
of surviving the Arctic to destroy himself with drink.
I don't want our audience out there to have to sit
listening to Johansen craving shots of *aquavit*.

And to be honest, Sybil, my Muse draws the line
at having crude four-letter words in anything of mine.

SYBIL THORNDIKE
Sorry!
  You and Nansen, such a diverse twain.
Strange that you were friends.

GILBERT MURRAY
     Allow me to explain.

Screen with UN emblem flown in.

I first met Fridtjof Nansen underneath this sign
representing, as it does, half his world and half mine.
That emblem up above me, he and I first met beneath –
the world from an odd angle enclosed with olive wreath.
The half I think as mine 's, of course, the wreath of
 peace,
representing what inspires me in the world of ancient
 Greece.
Nansen's half of the emblem is the skewed lopsided view
of the globe we're alarmed by because unaccustomed to.

SYBIL THORNDIKE
Why *is* the map lopsided and askew?

GILBERT MURRAY
It's the world as seen as if it's one united whole
but from the viewpoint of the nationless North Pole.
It amused Dr Nansen, the first man to have been
as near to the North Pole as 86 14,

that we first became acquainted underneath this sign
representing as it does half his world and half mine.

SYBIL THORNDIKE
Has Dr Fridtjof Nansen read anything by you?
If and when he sees his part will he know what to do?

GILBERT MURRAY
Dr Fridtjof Nansen is my most fervent fan!
Inordinately fond of poems that rhyme and scan!
Free verse appals him. He scorns the sort of Muse
that gives us rhymeless poetry like you-know-who's.
My verse, he assured me, was much to Nansen's liking
and him a man of action, an adventurer, a Viking!
Considered the most adventurous and glamorous man
     alive
when he almost reached the North Pole in 1895.
The complete man of action, a universal hero
who proved himself at temperatures of fifty below zero,
actually read and praised my verse translations.
He packed his head with poetry for Polar explorations.
You'd think a man of his kind, when he headed for the
     Pole,
would think about the body's needs and not about the
     soul,
but Nansen's shelves of poetry were packed inside his head
when only absolute necessities could be loaded on a sled.
Nansen's head 's replete with poems. I know none
     repleter.
He won't have any problems with Murray rhyme and
     metre.

SYBIL THORNDIKE
So while his many scenes show him expert in your verse,
if you can spare a moment, may we, *please*, rehearse?
And while Dr Nansen brings the Arctic into sight,
you, Gilbert Murray, have a lot of lines to write.

You're the last person needs reminding that in my long
    career
I have given my Clytemnestra, Hecuba, Medea.

Sybil Thorndike drags off Gilbert Murray, who rushes
back to retrieve the tragic Greek mask.
    Enter Nansen. A lantern-slide screen flies in. Poster
for FARTHEST NORTH. DR FRIDTJOF NANSEN.
LONDON.
    Nansen stands before the lantern-slide screen.

NANSEN

At your Royal Geographical Society in 1892
I lectured on my plans and heard those learned men
    pooh-pooh
my ideas for my journey and declare it wasn't true
that I could deduce an Arctic current from the seaman's
    oilskin garb
that had drifted from Siberia as far as Julianhaab
in south-west Greenland and so proved the current's flow.
I said there was a current. The RGS said no.
But I've not come back to London to say I told you so!
My success sprang from disaster. I owe a doleful debt
to the debris that had drifted from the doomed *Jeanette*
that sailed from San Francisco to the Bering Strait,
where it foundered, crushed by ice, a not uncommon fate
for ships in the Arctic ice pack. But from this wreck
    came clues.
The RGS said it couldn't change its (I thought rearguard)
    views
if the only evidence it was offered was a pair of oilskin
    trews.
They thought it was effrontery, the most impudent of
    cheeks
to think I'd alter Polar history with a pair of drifting
    breeks.

'And, look at the *Jeanette*,' they said. 'No ship can withstand
the crushing of the pack ice around Franz Josef Land.
When the temperature drops to forty below freezing
the ice pack round the Arctic ship begins its fatal squeezing.
and if the expedition meets such predictable defeat
Dr Nansen 's foolish to plan no line of retreat.'
They'd given me a medal for it so I didn't need to boast
I was first to cross Greenland from East coast to West coast,
from uninhabited to habited, so 'no line of retreat'
and it was now a strategy I intended to repeat.

Fram slide goes up on the screen.

FORWARD, FORWARD, Norwegian *Fram* 's the name
on my ship's prow. My heart 's stamped with the same.
And what a ship she proved to be, built with rounded sides
so when the groaning ice pack grips its hull it slides
downwards and the *Fram*, instead of cracking, lifts
and, frozen in the ice floes, as I predicted, drifts.

I had the best ship built that ever sailed the Polar Sea
and I left Christiania in 1893.
Some pompous 'expert' said, 'Nansen's going to lose
a lot more than the sailor who lost his oilskin trews.'
The 'experts' said that the ice would mash the *Fram*
to matchwood. I'd be doomed. And . . . and here I am!
in London to present some lantern slides which show
some of my adventures in the Arctic ice and snow.

A second lantern-slide screen with Fram. *Nansen moves to it.*

The 'experts' said that the ice would mash the *Fram*
to matchwood. I'd be doomed. And . . . and here I am!

in Newcastle to present some lantern slides which show
some of my adventures in the Arctic ice and snow.

A third and final lantern-slide screen with Fram.
Nansen moves to it.

The 'experts' said that the ice would mash the *Fram*
to matchwood. I'd be doomed. And . . . and here I am!
in Aberdeen to present some lantern slides which show
some of my adventures in the Arctic ice and snow.

All three screens still show the slide of the Fram. *As
Nansen shows his slides they appear simultaneously
on each screen.*

The *Fram* the very day I first felt the huskies pull
my sled towards the Pole. Note the rounded hull.
One of her special features that made her rise above
the pressure of the pack ice when the huge floes push
   and shove
and shatter ships less thoughtfully designed.
She gracefully glides upwards when the glaciers grind.
I left the *Fram* at latitude 84 4
uncertain when I left her if I'd see her any more.
It was March 14th 1895
and I struck out for the Pole determined to survive.
And –

A slide of Nansen's phonogram surrounded by ice.

   – although I had, reluctantly, to leave it on the *Fram*
I had the crew wind up my beloved phonogram
and place it on the ice so that it would play
Eva singing Grieg as the dog-sled pulled away.
This is my wife's voice pouring out her soul
fainter and fainter as I struck out for the Pole,
all art, all music, indeed anything refined
left, and maybe left for ever, far, far, far behind,
except for the poems I'd stored up in my mind.

And –

A slide of Hjalmar Johansen in Arctic furs appears on the screens.

– I want to introduce on this next lantern slide

The lantern-slide images of Johansen speak.

JOHANSEN
Hjalmar Johansen, drunk, depressive, suicide.

Nansen continues, totally unaware of the interruption. The lantern-slide images become still again.

NANSEN
my chosen companion on my quest for the Pole,
Hjalmar Johansen!

The lantern-slide images of Johansen speak.

JOHANSEN
The dark side of his soul!

The lantern-slide images of Johansen become still again. Nansen quickly moves the slide image onto one of dogs. The centre screen of the three still has the image of Johansen.

NANSEN
We made thorough preparations for our expedition:
dogs, loaded sleds, kayaks, guns and ammunition,
chocolate, pemmican, dehydrated soups by Knorr . . .

Nansen breaks off.

I hear you sentimental British, who put their dogs before
even other human beings, when I show this slide, say: 'Aw!'
In the whole of Europe no other group has sighed
so much in the darkness when I've shown this slide
of our faithful companions.

The image of Johansen speaks.

JOHANSEN
Tell them how they died!

NANSEN
(*as if not hearing*)
These were our most faithful companions and friends.

JOHANSEN
(*from the screen*)
Tell them how our 'companions' met their ends,
our huskies, our malamutes, our shaggy samoyeds.
Go on!

Nansen stays silent.

I wanted to put bullets through their heads
when they came to the end of their sled-hauling life.
But no! I was ordered to use my Lapland knife
and save bullets for bigger beasts that could provide
    more meat.
We gave the chopped-up huskies to the other dogs to
    eat.
Dr Nansen's a Darwinian with the stress on win!
We cut them up and fed the lumps to their surviving kin.
You could say that every dog was doubly employed,
as hauler of sled loads and dog's dinner when destroyed.
I doubt if canine qualms make hungry dogs demur
at cannibal consumption of a clapped-out comrade cur.
And maybe dogs have a more Darwinian drive
and gladly eat each other to keep themselves alive.
Maybe more Darwinian than Nansen who, though, likes
    to eat
husky blood in blubber as a special breakfast treat!

*Nansen angrily gets rid of the Johansen slide and the
slides of the dogs, and puts up one of a Norwegian
flag flying in a Polar wilderness.*

NANSEN

And that's our flag flying at 86 14,
the farthest northern latitude that anyone had been.
We'd hoped to reach the Pole but the drifting ice terrain
forced us finally to head back south again.
We ate a treat of chocolate, slept, and next day planned
to find the *terra firma* of Franz Josef Land.
We hadn't made the Pole but on this day we could boast
that, of all the people in the world, we were the
   northernmost.

Similar slide goes up with Norwegian flag in colour.

And here's a flag I coloured afterwards by hand
to show that it was Norway's flag that flew in that bleak
   land.
I carried colours in the Arctic which I had to sacrifice
to patch up our holed kayaks to get us through the ice.

But once the midnight sun had set we had to build
a winter hut and store up all the meat we'd killed
to survive the freezing darkness till the spring
made it once more possible to think of travelling.

*Another set of three lantern slides, this time forming a
continuous Polar landscape with, on one, a snow and
ice covered 'hut' as built by Nansen and Johansen
to survive the Arctic winter. On third slide (stage left)
the midnight sun begins to set and Johansen holds
out Nansen's Arctic gear as all the slides fly out
revealing the identical icy wilderness in 3D with a
'hut' and a setting midnight sun and Johansen holding
out Nansen's gear. Johansen helps Nansen into his
Arctic gear.*

NANSEN

This is the sort of layered bear-and-seal-fur gear
you're rarely ever out of as an Arctic pioneer.

Our clothes get blackened, caked with soot and greasy goo
and it gets pretty foetid in the sleeping bag for two.
The only occasions we get our hands and faces clean
is when we shoot a bear –

Johansen shoots his rifle at an offstage bear.

JOHANSEN
in all we shot nineteen.

NANSEN
And we can cut it open and do ablutions in the blood
that gushes from its body in a gratefully warm flood.
Our hut is ten feet long and exactly six feet wide.
The walls we made of stone and moss, the roof of
   walrus hide.
When I stretched my arms out my fingers touch each side.
There's an entrance like a burrow we crawl out and in
like an igloo with a door of double walrus skin.
We'll sleep all hours, twenty out of twenty-four
and we'll be able to sleep singly as we couldn't do before.

The midnight sun sets, leaving moonlit darkness.

Right, Johansen!
                 Our winter lodgings are complete.
I'll be free of your snoring and your fidgeting feet.
We've got long months of Arctic winter to get through
and I won't sleep at all if I've still to sleep with you!
You're always twitching and what's more upsetting
   you're a
persistently objectionable trombone-volume snorer.
Now we've got our hut constructed, what I really want
   to do
's divide the bag we've had to share right now into two.
Now we can have our separate spaces, one bag each,
with the cooker in the middle that both of us can reach.
I can't bear to be so close to you when you start to snore.

> JOHANSEN
> (*under breath*)

And the poetry you keep muttering 's a total bloody bore.

> NANSEN

What's that?

> JOHANSEN

We should have done this long before.

> NANSEN

Not possible in the little tent, too cramped and poky, but
now we can be expansive in our palatial hut.
Not to have to listen to you when you snore and fart!

> JOHANSEN

Or to you when you're spouting the poet's putrid art.

> NANSEN

What was that, Johansen?

> JOHANSEN

I said let's make a start.
It's easy to split it. We'll divide it down the seams.

> NANSEN

Tonight I'm looking forward to slightly sweeter dreams.

*They enter the hut. A 'night' elapses. A green Aurora.
Hjalmar Johansen emerges, trembling with cold. Then
after a while Nansen, also shivering, though trying to
hide the fact. Nansen's clothes and face are now as
black and greasy as Johansen's. Neither wants to admit
that they couldn't sleep in their separate sleeping bags.*

> NANSEN

Ah, Johansen, slept a good deal better, I've no doubt?

> JOHANSEN

Like an innocent baby, sir. Went right out.

NANSEN

Me too. Wonderful not to have to hear you snore.

JOHANSEN

In my own space I slept much better than before.

Pause.

NANSEN

I think you're a liar. You didn't sleep all night.

JOHANSEN

To be honest, Dr Nansen, you're absolutely right.

NANSEN

I was frozen. Didn't sleep a wink. In such sub-zero
    weather
we don't have a choice. Sew the two bits back together.

Exit Nansen into hut.

JOHANSEN

In separate bags we spent a freezing sleepless night
and there's nothing really for it except glumly reunite.

Exit Johansen into the hut.
    The Aurora Borealis with spectacular purple light.
    Enter Nansen to contemplate the Aurora. He begins
sketching the phenomenon with a box of pastel crayons.

NANSEN

It's a great relief to escape that farter and that snorer
and get my spirits lifted by the sight of the Aurora.
The sagas say that fire-giant Surt 's the one who plays
this lyre strung with light, this veil of purple rays,
the strings that sparkle in the flames of Muspelheim
that represent to Vikings the end of human time.
The fire-giant Surt plays his luminescent lyre
to serenade the world's end in the final fire.
Surt plucks solemn dirges from the last auroral rays

shimmering for the last men in the world's last days.
But as a modern scientific Viking I know the cooling sun
will make the world's finale a far more frozen one.

*Nansen continues contemplating the Aurora and
sketching.*
  *Enter Johansen. He starts picking up the pastels
and testing them.*

What are you doing, Johansen?

JOHANSEN
                    Seeing if they'll do.

NANSEN
Do for what? Drawing's never interested you.

JOHANSEN
The kayaks are leaking. Your sketching chalk,
ground up and mixed with blubber, 'd make good kayak
  caulk.

NANSEN
Ground up? They're far too precious to me whole
to capture the Aurora that captivates my soul.

JOHANSEN
If you ever want us to escape out of the ice
you'll have to face up to that artistic sacrifice.

NANSEN
I know you took against me because of, I think, the fact
that instead of extra pemmican you noticed that I'd
  packed
my sketching pads and pastels. Do you resent
the life of the finer spirit my pastels represent?

JOHANSEN
The mandate in our packing was, only carry gear
utterly essential to the Polar pioneer,

94

and for me it wasn't essential, hardly vital
to lug along a phonogram with your wife's song recital.
I'd wanted my accordion and a little *aquavit*,
both essential to my spirit, that you did not permit.

NANSEN

To make you less grudging and embittered I left the
    phonogram
with Eva singing Grieg's songs back on board the *Fram*.

JOHANSEN

You had it playing on the ice as we departed.

NANSEN

I couldn't bear to leave her voice. I was broken-hearted.

JOHANSEN

I know the tune by heart. I heard you play
Eva singing Edvard Grieg almost every day.
I know you're the commander. If you say 'Art supplies
are fundamental', who am I to criticise?
But now, Dr Nansen, I'm afraid you have to choose
between sketching the Aurora or caulking our canoes.
We'll never get through the ice floes if your precious art
    supply
isn't pounded up with blubber to keep our kayaks dry.

NANSEN
(*looking at the Aurora*)
How can you hope to capture that fantastic light
in photographs that show it in only black and white?

*Nansen throws down pastels and flaunts off angrily
back into the hut.*
    *Johansen starts grinding the pastels with great
relish, pounding them rhythmically. An Aurora flashes
spectacularly and dies away.*

JOHANSEN

Well, I felt a bit triumphant when his precious art supply
got pounded up with blubber to keep our kayaks dry.
The crayons were essential to caulk the kayak leaks.
We'll need them, I hope, soon, but Nansen's sulked for
    weeks.
I thought it just a ruse he used so he didn't have to talk,
drawing the Aurora with his pretty artist's chalk.
Now the ruse he'll use more of 'll be declaiming verse.
He'll do almost anything so we won't converse.
Reciting poetry! Something he preferred
to speaking to me to whom he scarcely said a word.

   Imitating Nansen:

'The only spiritual equivalent I myself have found
to six pounds of beefsteak sun-and-wind-dried to one
    pound
is, Johansen, poetry, the spirit's pemmican,
that nourishes the soul as no other substance can.
Until we escape from here, until that happy day,
the pemmican of poetry will be my spirit's stay.
Poetry, Johansen, not I fancy to your taste,
is now my only consolation in this Arctic waste.'

   Exit Johansen into the hut.
      *Time elapses. Another Aurora lights up the sky
briefly and dies.*
      *Nansen pushes the double bear-fur bag out of the
hut.*

NANSEN

This double bear-fur bag that you and I are sharing
stinks of farts and blubber and badly needs an airing.

   *Johansen bashes the bag to clear it of ice and the
rhythm gradually becomes that of the metre of the
verse he and Nansen are speaking.*

96

JOHANSEN

In this double bear-fur bag with its blubber smells and
    farts
I had my reluctant schooling in the skaldic arts.
We had to share the bear-fur bag to keep our bodies warm
and his nocturnal chunterings taught me poetic form.
In this double bear-fur bag where our bodies really stink,
me, I just lay there, desperate, listening, and I think
how much bloody longer till I can get a bloody drink.

*Johansen bangs on the double bear-fur bag to relieve
his frustration.*

And if there was a respite from the sound of verse
the rare conversations were, frankly, a lot worse.
One particular one I remember really fucked my brain.

*Enter Nansen, who surveys the vast icy landscape.
He helps to hold up the fur sleeping bag for Johansen
to bang.*

NANSEN

The whole globe will become like this ice-bound bleak
    terrain!
This icy landscape we endure, great scientists have said,
will be global, universal, once the sun is dead!
You know, Johansen, science prophesies
the whole globe will be polar once the sun's fire dies.
It's a certainty, Johansen, Man cannot rely
on the sun being eternal. One day the sun will die.
Humanity will die with temperatures so low
and it will mean the end of everything we know.
The whole Earth, even the tropics, will finally appear
as white and as frozen as the land around us here.
Then the world will scrabble for sleeping bags like these!
Furless unfortunates will be the first to freeze.

JOHANSEN

But what if humanity could co-operate
and collectively save the doomed globe from this fate?
There's Socialism some men start believing in . . .

NANSEN

Socialism, Johansen, 's pathetic, feminine.

JOHANSEN

Sorry, Dr Nansen, just thought it worth a mention.

NANSEN

Socialism's an inconceivable contravention
of the basic rules of life which, Darwin says, require
that the weaker should always sink beneath the higher.
And when the sun does cool and the last days come,
even if it's not till next millennium,
you can bet your so-called socialists will fight
their erstwhile comrades for food and heat and light.
Until in the end there'll be no way to sustain
life on Earth's frozen surface.

Exit Nansen.

JOHANSEN
                              Yeah, that fucked my brain.
Nansen's idea of chit-chat or bedtime conversation
conjuring up the vision of the globe's annihilation,
I think that that belief of his helped put into my head
that life had no purpose and I was better dead.
The Earth's ultimate extinction! Makes you think
why bother living, struggling, and that drives you to drink.
But he won't permit it here, and it's rather fucking far
to trek across the Arctic to find a bloody bar.

So take a look! This view you've got before you 's how
the whole globe's going to look not too long from now.
The whole globe, seas and cities, Paris, Berlin, Rome,

the frozen neighbourhood about your London home –
Hampstead, Islington, the West End, the South Bank,
all a featureless, completely frozen blank.
It robs the heart of purpose, saps the spirit's goals
to know the globe in its entirety will end up like the poles.
Even Darwin's fittest 'll be no better placed
for survival than the weakest in the final frozen waste.
The fittest will seem feeble and the fittest of the fit
like 'Farthest North' Nansen and the Arctic Inuit,
used as they may be to the Polar ice and snow,
will find that even they die at temperatures so low.

When I walk this ice and snow I'm inside my own brain
which is a similar barren ice-bound bleak terrain.
But if that bastard had allowed it and I could only pour a
nice big glass of *aquavit* I'd make my own Aurora,
and feel the fiery spirit give me a certain glow
deep in the grateful gut, and fuck the ice and snow.
But the only bit of warmth I'll get round here is back
with bloody Nansen in this bloody bear-fur sack.

> *Exit Johansen, pulling the double bear-fur bag behind
> him into hut.*
> *Arctic winter over. Sun. Enter Nansen and Johansen
> from hut. They start to leave and set off dragging
> kayaks.*

When we have to use our kayaks when it's too wet to
  walk
you'll be glad I used your crayons to make the kayak
  caulk.
Patched with pastels I pounded to make a pitchy glue
instead of pretty pictures of auroras that you drew.
If I hadn't done it then the kayaks would've sunk
and you'd never get a chance to compete with Edvard
  Munch.
And look, the last of these auroras –

99

NANSEN

Aurorae!

JOHANSEN

Whatever! I'll remember them until the day I die.

NANSEN

That day could well be sooner than you think.

JOHANSEN

I refuse to die till I've had a good stiff drink.
I've dreamed for all this time about that first big dram.

NANSEN

And I of home, my armchair, and my phonogram.
And reuniting with our comrades from the *Fram*.

> *They travel, hauling the kayaks. They stop.*
> *Time elapses. Johansen fires his rifle at some animal*
> *for food. Sound of dogs barking.*

Johansen, barking dogs. And barking dogs mean men.
Perhaps we are going to see our motherland again.

> *A mass of Norwegian flags.* Fram *comes into*
> *Christiania Harbour projected onto Olivier shutters.*
> *Sound of brass bands and cheering.*
> *Enter Gilbert Murray, and Sybil Thorndike in her*
> *dressing gown.*

GILBERT MURRAY

Home to brass bands and cheering on the Christiania
quays.

SYBIL THORNDIKE

Thank God, you didn't want me sliding in on skis!
Even I, not a veggie, soon had quite enough
of the bears' brains and the blubber and the *Boys Own
Paper* stuff.
I'm so relieved you didn't force me to appear

in that positively unflattering greasy polar gear.
For one awful moment I thought you'd brought me
    back
to enter Larry's theatre in some ghastly anorak.
Long ago I made myself a golden rule:
never play a character whose costume's a kagool.
It must have made you nauseous, the meat whiffs from
    the hut.

GILBERT MURRAY

I feared they'd start gutting seals so kept my eyes tight
    shut.
I'll watch the crowds cheer Nansen, Nansen being feted,
but would rather not watch Johansen get inebriated.
Nansen has an audience with King Oscar.

JOHANSEN
(*shouting off*)
                              Forget that Oscar shit!
Christiania will see me quaffing *aquavit*.

GILBERT MURRAY

Everywhere in Europe there was a Nansen 'boom'
as Johansen's dram indulgences brought him nearer doom.
For a short time he broke his dependence on the 'dram'
and Nansen got Johansen back on board the *Fram*
as a member of Amundsen's expedition crew,
a chance the bibulous beggar belligerently blew
when, after immoderate imbibing, and an insubordinate
    act,
Captain Amundsen had Johansen summarily sacked.
Which put paid to the ambition the doomed dram-bibber
    nursed
of triumphing over Nansen by reaching a Pole first.
The dismissal turned him into a melancholy loner
stoked up on *aquavit* and always short of *kroner*.
Nansen's northern record lasted only for five years

before being superseded by other Polar pioneers.
He began to drift directionless into dark grudge and grief.

SYBIL THORNDIKE
Sounds like it needs me to bring some light relief.

Exit Gilbert Murray and Sybil Thorndike.
Enter Nansen to chair and phonogram.

NANSEN
I was the man reached latitude 86 14,
the farthest north that any man had ever been,
but the record only lasted five brief years
before being overtaken by new Polar pioneers.
The double, hurtful irony 's that what were once my ships
helped Amadeo and Amundsen to accomplish my eclipse.
Jason, the sealer I sailed to Greenland in, became
Amadeo's *Pole Star* and put paid to my fame.
My *Jason* got Amadeo further North than me.
I'd reached 86 14 and Amadeo 33.
Twenty miles only, but twenty's all it needed
for me to know my record was safely superseded.

Reads telegram:

OBJECTIVE REACHED STOP AMUNDSEN. That put a
    stop to me
being at the pinnacle of polar history.
My own Arctic achievements seem more and more remote
now Amundsen's reached the South Pole using *Fram*,
    my boat.
Amundsen reached the South Pole with such apparent ease
because he used my system of sledges, dogs and skis.
I was once more among crowds on the Christiania quay,
crowds cheering their new hero, but this time it's not me.

Fram once more sails into Christiania Harbour with
brass bands and waving flags.

Enter Hjalmar Johansen, drunk.

JOHANSEN

It was almost, but for Amundsen, me the quayside throng
would have been cheering in the *Fram* where I belong,
me, the second time *Fram* voyager Norwegians would
    applaud
but *Fram* sailed up the fjord and I was not on board.
Amundsen, the bastard who sacked me, used your boat
for his conquest of the South Pole and is going to demote
the name of Nansen on the roster of the great
when the fickle voice of fame finds newer names to
    celebrate.
For five years everywhere you've been cheered and feted.
What future after Amundsen now you've been relegated?
A Darwinist with the stress on win. So what happens
    when you lose?
Does it make you open to more sympathetic views?
Can you look into your heart and find some empathy
with those destined to be losers, like me, like me, like me?

Nansen in his depressed reverie puts on the
phonogram: his wife Eva singing Grieg. He listens.

NANSEN

Eva! whose voice I still listen to on the phonogram
as I did in the Arctic winter before we left the *Fram*.
It consoles me to listen. Though she's dead I still need her
though the consolation I need now is way beyond all
    lieder.
With the globe entirely penetrated, both poles mapped,
it leaves me with my energy completely sapped.
The conquered poles have paralysed my initiative
and without my urge for action I find it hard to live.
I feel surrounded by ice floes but this time they're all
    black,
implacable, crushing, and my heart's about to crack.

The heart I thought was like the *Fram* is more like the
    Jeanette,
crushed by the icy darkness though not quite shattered yet.
Despair makes me dispirited, listless and unmanned
as much as poor Johansen –

> *The sound of Eva's singing grows.*
>   *Bang. It's Johansen, whom we see shoot himself.*
> *A great spurt of blood spouts onto the ice.*
> *Enter Ghost of Johansen.*

JOHANSEN

                         – who died by his own hand.
You thought it and I did it, as if at your command!
I blew my brains out with the very gun I shot
bears and seals and foxes for our supper pot.
Like the pennants of blood sprayed from our polar prey,
my brains were hauled and flown in exactly the same way.
I've seen it so many times but now the flag that's flown
and the brains that burst out with it are no beast's but
    my own,
a blast of flapping banner, a gory banderole,
a bloodflag with the blazon of my brain-sick blackened
    soul.
That bloodflag of my suicide should be planted to be seen
by all who reach the wilderness of 86 14.

I put into practice what you scarcely dared to think.
You want solace for your sorrow, but Johansen quaffs
    the drink.
You saw the unmapped places conquered one by one
and felt your life was pointless but Johansen fires the gun.
You thought the desperate thought. I did the deed.
I didn't damn my spirit so Nansen's could be freed,
freed to find some other soul-fulfilling goal
to compensate your spirit for the conquest of the Pole.
This act of mine, this suicide, it's meant always to bind

your thoughts and my thoughts together in one mind.
When I blew my brains out it was not to make you free
but bind you even closer to the ghost that once was me.

NANSEN

My spirit was almost crushed but like the *Fram* in frozen
    floes,
gripped by despair and darkness, withstood their force,
    and rose.
The sun will cool, the Earth will freeze, that simple fact,
though it paralysed Johansen, now makes me want to act.
The Earth will be one huge Arctic and man's endeavour
disappear beneath the ice and lost to time for ever.
You've got to steel your mind and heart to gaze into that
    void
and then commit to action and be busily employed.
We create our purpose, we create our goal.
And now it's helping humankind, not reaching the
    North Pole.
Science says its certain, Johansen's desperate reaction
was drink, depresssion, suicide, mine was always *action*.

    Exit Nansen.

JOHANSEN

My last action was the fatal shot, but if he acts or no
everywhere that Nansen goes my ghost will also go.
My ghost swears never to leave Nansen's side
and haunt the lapsed Darwinian with my suicide,
League of Nations Commissioner for Refugees!
Not a post a Darwinian can fulfil with any ease!
I'll be there to denounce the doctor for his Darwinian
    defection.
It's not Nature now but Nansen who is doing the selection.
Now that he's adopted his international role
he's jettisoned those laws of life we clung to at the Pole.
Johansen's ghost returns to put back in his ear

all he wants suppressing in his new world-wide career.
I'll remind him, ex-Darwinian, what he drummed into
    my brain –
the strong should flourish, the weak go down the drain.
He's a 'humanitarian' now, no longer an explorer
and he's off to New York to watch a ballet called *Aurora*.

Sound of an orchestra tuning up.
    Gold proscenium, red velvet curtains fly in.

Composer, designer, dancer, each a Russian émigré,
came on so-called 'Nansen passports' to the USA.
But did any Nansen-passport-saved Pied Piper with his
    flute
do anything to civilise the European brute?
Although the bloody ballet's something I can't bear
I want to sour his delight with a dose of my despair.
Despair a gift from you that I will give you back
to remind you of the darkness when we shared one
    sleeping sack.

Exit Johansen.
    *Enter Gilbert Murray through red curtains. He
    tiptoes downstage to lean over the 'orchestra pit'.*

GILBERT MURRAY
Maestro! Maestro! For the purpose of my play
could you give us a rendition of only part of the ballet?

*Spotlight on curtain. The head of Sybil Thorndike
pokes through.*

SYBIL THORNDIKE
So before I appear there's a whole ballet to sit through?

GILBERT MURRAY
I've already told the orchestra a part of it will do.

SYBIL THORNDIKE
Then me?

GILBERT MURRAY

Yes, you, and me, and Nansen, London, 1922.
We'll meet him and others and sit in on their discussions
on how they can publicise the plight of starving Russians.

Exit Gilbert Murray through red curtains.

SYBIL THORNDIKE
(*to Gilbert Murray*)
I can't wait much longer!

To audience:

Well, at least he's let you know
you won't have long to wait before the real star of the
show.

Exit Sybil Thorndike.
   The curtain rises.
   *The scene is the same Arctic wilderness, except it is
now framed by a gilded proscenium arch for the ballet
of the Aurora Borealis, a ballet that should seem as if
composed by Stravinsky, designed by Chagall and
danced by Pavlova, all of whom were recipients at
one time or another of a Nansen passport.*
   *There are also two theatre boxes. In one sits
Fridtjof Nansen.*

*The ballet ends. Dancer takes her call. Curtsies to
Nansen in box. Nansen presents a bouquet of red
roses to the Dancer. Applause. Curtain.*
   Exit Nansen, revealing Johansen behind.
   *Johansen changes the box into one at the Bolshoi
with hammer and sickle over the old double eagle of
the Tsar.*

JOHANSEN

Now he's going back to Russia to tour the famine zone
acting as if he's feeding the millions on his own.

My ghost'll be on his trail, and always ready to remind
Nansen the Darwinist of beliefs he's left behind.

Johansen sees ARA Men entering their box.

On furlough from the famine for a bit of Moscow play,
here come the youthful heroes of the ARA,
the American Relief Administration,
doing even more than Nansen to relieve starvation,
having time off from the famine, a free box at the Bolshoi.
Each one, except their Moscow boss, nobbut a green boy
from the boondocks of Iowa, Wisconsin, Illinois.

Three ARA Men, Stuart Shaw, James Callaghan and
William H. Rutland, enter their box in the middle of
a discussion which continues while they doff their fur
hats and coats.

STUART SHAW
What you're saying's wrong. If you think that you're a
    fool.
Finishing the famine won't prop up Bolshie rule.

JAMES CALLAGHAN
Hoover wouldn't do it if he thought that was true
and I wouldn't be here helping . . .

WILLIAM H. RUTLAND
                                    and nor would you.
The one thing that's been paradoxically essential 's
Hoover's utterly impeccable anti-Bolshevik credentials.
Herbert Hoover's always, always, you know, presumed
that the folly of communism 's ultimately doomed.
I've always understood it was Hoover's attitude
that the Russian Revolution was a riot about food.

STUART SHAW
Somewhere the basic ethos of Hoover's ARA 's
if you want to stop Bolshevism, food's the best of ways.

The American Relief Administration 's a manoeuvre
typical of the genius of our Chief, Herbert Hoover.

WILLIAM H. RUTLAND

He's had to square our save-the-starving mission
with US official policy of complete non-recognition.
The Bolshies' bungling and the bureaucratic mess
would be seen in total contrast with ARA success
and efficiency, all down to the Chief,
Herbert Hoover, the genius of famine relief.

JAMES CALLAGHAN

The ARA makes Bolshevism seem like a dead loss.

STUART SHAW

Here comes Sheldon, guys, the Moscow bureau boss.

*An older man, Sheldon, enters the box and struggles
out of his furs.*

SHELDON

Thank God tonight's an opera. I've had it with ballet.
Not that Isadora does it in the normal way.
I saw her here in Moscow perform to a great crowd.
If I wasn't among VIPs I'd've laughed out loud.
She danced *The Russian Famine*. What arrogance
for this podgy passé prancer to do a *Famine* dance.
She pranced about in skimpy silks to a Scriabin *étude*.
All I can say is, thank Christ she wasn't dancing nude!
Rolls of blubber round the belly somehow don't symbolise
starvation on the Volga, not to mention chubby thighs!
I thought, for Christ's sake, keep all the arts away
from the kind of work we try to do in the ARA,
especially preserve us from the art of the ballet.
So thank God it's an opera we got tickets for tonight.

Hey, look behind the hammer and sickle of the USSR,
you can still see the great gold double eagle of the Tsar.
And that's the Tsar's own box! Oh my Gawd!

A Man in furs enters the Tsar's box.

Look, there!

Man in box removes furs and reveals himself as Nansen.

JAMES CALLAGHAN
Who is it?

SHELDON
Nansen! Just wait, they'll all applaud.

Long applause and cheers from unseen audience.
Nansen bows and waves.

WILLIAM H. RUTLAND
I had a letter from my folks back home, by the way,
saying Nansen was responsible for improving our ballet.
They saw one in New York entitled *The Aurora*
and said it owed so much to Nansen the explorer-
turned-humanitarian and were full of praise
about the boost to arts there'd been with all the émigrés
on Nansen passports, glad, no doubt, to have fled
the famine here in Russia and the diet of dung bread.

SHELDON
I've a meeting in London, England, with our very man,
a kinda famine summit for this year's master plan.
We'll be meeting in a coupla days to sum up and review
our Russian famine strategy for 1922.
The other agencies, *Save the Children*, *Society of Friends*,
who are giving us what help they can to achieve our ends,
they'll be there represented by a Miss Jebb and Miss Fry
at whom I've no doubt Nansen will be rolling the old eye!
And there'll be Gilbert Murray, a League of Nations type,
who'll probably contribute some idealistic tripe.
Hoover's American Relief Administration 's
going to achieve far more than any League of Nations.
The ARA has set up an efficient working model

for famine relief; we don't need League of Nations
  twaddle.
And this Professor Murray so I'm told 's a drama freak.
Drama would be bad enough but his kind 's ancient
  Greek!
He's partial to Greek drama in his own translations
and more naive than Nansen about the League of Nations.
Murray 's escorting, as his special lady guest,
some broad called Sybil Thorndike, said to be the best
actress of her generation. God! We're gonna have to sit
and listen to her declaiming ancient tragic shit.

JAMES CALLAGHAN
Don't envy you that. Can't imagine anything worse
than have to hear some British broad spouting fucking
  verse!

*Applause from Bolshoi audience as Conductor enters
to begin the overture.*

SHELDON
Oop, here comes the conductor. I dunno. I dunno
what good's going to come from being at this show.
I'd better shut up. It's about to start.
Once you've seen the famine you wonder about art!

Applause. Conductor. Overture.
  *Overture finishes. Red velvet curtain of the Bolshoi
goes up to reveal Eglantyne Jebb watching the* Save
the Children Fund *film of the Russian famine.*
  *It ends, then she switches on the lights of a room of
her house turned into a kind of campaign centre, and
she broods about the film until the spool of film runs
out of the projector.*
  The gold proscenium flies out.
  *Sheldon in London on his way to a meeting with
Fridtjof Nansen, Gilbert Murray, Sybil Thorndike,
Eglantyne Jebb and Ruth Fry.*

SHELDON

Though we've both worked on the famine, I regret
that Nansen and I have not, till now in London, ever met.
Nansen, Miss Jebb, Miss Fry the Quaker, and the prof –
what's his name, Professor Murray! I shouldn't scoff,
I guess, and I know he's also a League of Nations man
who is earnest and committed to doing what he can,
but how can Greek drama be of any earthly use
to us in famine work? OK, so maybe I'm a bit obtuse,
but I figure he's got that actress Sybil-something in tow
because he's planning on performing some after-dinner
    show.
The reality in this canister is gonna supersede
All that poetry-spouting, Sybil Thorndike breed.
God spare us goddam culture when the point of our
    discussion 's
the quickest way to save the lives of millions of Russians.

Nansen towers above us, although the ARA
feeds millions more than he could in a single day.
We do all the goddam work and he gets the applause.

Enter Nansen, Gilbert Murray, Sybil Thorndike,
Eglantyne Jebb and Ruth Fry.

SHELDON

Dr Nansen, my hero, the inspiration of our cause!
I feel so honoured to meet you here today

NANSEN

You're working on the Volga with the ARA?

SHELDON

Yes, sir, Sheldon, and we're all inspired by you.

NANSEN

That would be wonderful if it were only true.

SHELDON

How could you ever doubt it? Surely you're aware

of how you're applauded for the work you've done out
    there?
You've taught the world compassion, the indifferent to
    care.

EGLANTYNE JEBB
The indifferent need to learn to care a good deal more
and that, dear Dr Nansen, 's what your Queen's Hall
    lecture's for.
Mr Sheldon, pleased to meet you. Miss Jebb, Eglantyne!

NANSEN
We all have a favourite flower, and the eglantine,
with its slightly timid beauty, happens to be mine.

GILBERT MURRAY
Miss Jebb, your bloodstream must be full of ancient
    Greece.

To all:

She is the greatest editor of Sophocles's niece.
Miss Jebb, you may be, but our guests are unaware
I succeeded your uncle Richard to the Glasgow chair.

EGLANTYNE JEBB
I know my uncle Richard was your predecessor
in the Chair of Greek at Glasgow. I welcome you,
    Professor!

GILBERT MURRAY
(to Sheldon, the ARA man)
I'm Professor Murray.

Introduces Sybil Thorndike.

                    And this Sybil Thorndike, a sensation
as Hecuba . . .

SYBIL THORNDIKE
in Dr Murray's own translation!

GILBERT MURRAY

She is what you Americans refer to as a 'star'.

SHELDON

I've not had the privilege of seeing you so far.
Perhaps you'd grace the evening with a recitation.
Sheldon! American Relief Administration.

SYBIL THORNDIKE

Good evening, Mr Sheldon, I think your ARA
and Dr Nansen do far more than any play.

EGLANTYNE JEBB

Sybil, we all try our best, each in our own way.
We all look forward to hearing your ideas tonight
how theatre can help the starving in their sorry plight.

To everybody:

Everybody! We need to check if the nationwide
  discussion 's
swinging in our favour in the matter of the Russians.
Let's review the papers then we'll go next door to eat.
Dr Nansen, there's one more guest for you to meet –

Eglantyne Jebb ushers Ruth Fry before Nansen.

A guest whom I think you may already know.

NANSEN
(*approving the look of Ruth Fry*)
I'm not sure that I do. But would dearly wish it so!

EGLANTYNE JEBB

I can't believe you've not already met.

NANSEN
(*using his doubt to look Ruth Fry over*)
I don't think that we have. Much to my regret.

EGLANTYNE JEBB

Ruth Fry! Of *The Friends*! She was on the Volga too.

NANSEN

One meets so many people, but I'm sorry I missed you.

RUTH FRY

Dr Nansen! It's an honour. How do you do?

EGLANTYNE JEBB

So now we'll review the papers and dream up means
   to try
to publicise the famine before more millions die.

Gilbert Murray holds up the Greek mask.

GILBERT MURRAY

Before we get too deeply into our deliberation
I should like to make beforehand a little presentation.
Dr Nansen, this gift is for you. The tragic mask!
To give you inspiration for your momentous task.
Inspiration from the ancient past, to help you stir and
   shake
those who need persuading, for the starving millions' sake,
to lend first their attention, then their financial aid.

NANSEN

I'll need it. Europe's far from easy to persuade.

GILBERT MURRAY

The tragic mask for me has come to symbolise
the art of facing horror with always-open eyes.
No eyelids on a tragic mask. It has no choice but see
and its mouth is always open to utter poetry.

NANSEN

The mouth of starvation is always open too.

GILBERT MURRAY

But our mask's ancient eloquence will help inspire you
to move the world to end the famine, but I think it's only
   right
that you should receive it from our theatre's leading light.

SYBIL THORNDIKE

From the bottom of my heart and from thespians
  nationwide
who would all desert the stage to do service at your side,
from all of us in theatre who do the little that we can
our token of regard to a most inspiring man.
Please accept this present as a mark of our esteem.

Nansen contemplates the mask and Sybil Thorndike.
He puts it to his face and screams very loud. Everyone
is shocked. Nansen laughs.

NANSEN

It reminds me of my countryman Edvard Munch's *The*
  Scream.
For well nigh thirty years the picture's haunted me,
painted as it was by Munch in 1893,
the same year, indeed almost to the day,
the *Fram* went down the fjord about to sail away.
There's a boat in the background and I think there I am
at the start of my adventure in the departing *Fram.*
It looks like Christiania, but the earth, the sea, the sky
are all vibrating with the violence of the cry.
And since being in the Volga I have terrifying dreams
of the open mouths of hunger and the open mouths of
  screams.
In the Volga there are millions of open mouths like these
who need substantial sustenance, not your Euripides.

GILBERT MURRAY

We've raised money and subscribers to the League of
  Nations
by playing the most popular of my Euripides translations,
The Trojan Women with Sybil in the lead.

NANSEN

                                        Murray, yes.
But do you really think poetry's the right thing to address
the horrors we are witnessing in times like these,

horrors quite unknown to your friend Euripides?
You know I value poetry quite as much as you:
I survived the Arctic winter by reciting poems I knew,
but could your Greek tragedians, even if they speak
the brilliant English you found for all their Greek,
ever hope to accomplish a poetical narration
of the plight of millions threatened by starvation?
Surely even your tragedians would be bound to fail
to put into poetry a horror on this scale.

GILBERT MURRAY

I'm sure they could. O how I wish that I
really had the talent to give the task a try.
But as a certain someone 's been unkind enough to say,
poetry's not Professor Murray's principal forte.
and many agree with a certain someone's views
on the outmoded melodies of Gilbert Murray's Muse.

EGLANTYNE JEBB

I'd like to begin with what I'm certain you all here
will regard as yet another crazy Eglantyne idea!
What we need at *Save the Children* is a way
that can communicate the horror that language can't
    convey.
Can you imagine, Dr Nansen, your slide-projection screen
as a permanent mural in a crowded works canteen?
What would happen to the world if lantern slides could be
projected into people's homes while they were having tea?
If these actualities could be seen by the whole nation
surely it would mean an end to the horrors of starvation.
If we had a sort of visual version of the telephone
with every household owning a small screen of its own,
I know it seems far-fetched but I know that we'd persuade
people with a 'vision phone' to contribute to aid.
If only we could *see* like we hear on radio,
a wireless that as well as tell could also show.
There'd be no more starvation like this in Saratov.

GILBERT MURRAY

Eglantyne, they might just simply switch it off.

EGLANTYNE JEBB
(*picks up newspaper*)

Look here! We've used this drawing to juxtapose
half-naked Volga starving to our sort in fine clothes.
But my committee thought I'd gone too far when I
     proposed
far more shocking contrasts to be juxtaposed:
a peasant, next to a family weighed down with Christmas
     shopping,
excavating strands of straw from a steaming carthorse
     dropping.
'Good taste' forbids it. 'Good taste' 's my worst frustration.
What on earth is 'tasteful' about extreme starvation?
We at *Save the Children* haven't shied from the technique
that advertising uses, letting pictures speak.

She picks up another paper.

We'll have this advert in the paper. The headline's going
     to say
in large capitals: DOOMED TO DIE ON XMAS DAY.
In the short time it takes to munch a Michaelmas mince pie
a hundred starving Russian mites are going to surely die.
If I had my way, I'd dump all that good taste and adopt
shock tactics that are certain to get starvation stopped.
One day, not now, but one day when we can
show the horrors of Samara and Saratov and Kazan
in all their ghastly colour and hear the children's cries,
we'll succeed in ending famine. I hate this compromise.

NANSEN

'Compromise is Satan's work.' Henrik Ibsen, *Brand*!

EGLANTYNE JEBB

Yes, dear Dr Nansen, I know you understand.

RUTH FRY

Of course it has to be admitted that the most acute distress
is not in Russia but in Cornwall, or so says the *Express*.

She picks up the Express.

Look, columns on Cornwall and the paper's damning
on the Volga which they call 'the other famine'.
Lord Beaverbrook's *Express*! There's a pernicious *exposé*
of you at *Save the Children* in the *Express* every day!
Beaverbrook's readers have their tender feelings torn
by unemployed tin-miners in Redruth or Camborne.

EGLANTYNE JEBB

Our rubbishers on Beaverbrook's *Express* contend
that we (that of course means me) at *Save the Children*
   spend
more on salaries and adverts and administration
than goes in the end to Russia to relieve starvation.
Our patron, the Archbishop of Canterbury no less,
has also been vilified in this week-old *Express*.

Reads from the Express:

'The Archbishop would do best to distribute
charitable food to his Lambeth destitute.
Never mind the Volga, he only needs to take his walks
in the slums of Lambeth to see where Famine stalks.'

NANSEN

And this is me from an issue of last week.
As a kind of culmination to their usual critique
of how unbelievable my last reports had been,
the *Express* invites its readers to judge between
the words of a 'foreigner' (that's me!) and what's been
   written
by 'an *Express* journalist born and bred in Britain'.
We've got to use cunning and contrive new ways to
   counteract
the Beaverbrook *Express* and show the famine's fact.

When they attacked the famine as a Bolshevistic lie
all I could do to silence them was *verbally* deny,
but from now on in Russia the photographs I take
will be the proof I need to show the famine isn't fake.
Express readers will believe Beaverbrook's foul lies
until they see the starving before their very eyes,
and it's that in the end that has forced me to decide
I had once more to resort to the realistic slide.
Perhaps 'movies' will become the more realistic means
of convincing an audience they're seeing actual scenes.
Miss Jebb, or may I call you Eglantyne,
it happens to be a favourite flower of mine,
you at Save the Children are there already, are you not?
Your director and myself were (what's the parlance?) . . .

SHELDON

'shot'.

EGLANTYNE JEBB

We'll watch our film and Mr Sheldon's later. Film's a new
and important way to get our message through.
Oue film's been shown already on more than one occasion.
A wonderful new weapon in our armoury of persuasion.
So, Dr Nansen, I agree that you are right
to be showing slides of horror in your talk tomorrow
    night.
I think we'll find such methods will be more and more
    employed –
the saviour of the starving may well be celluloid.

RUTH FRY

But sometimes it *is* possible the camera can lie.

NANSEN

Don't tell that to Beaverbrook, I beg of you, Miss Fry!
Since his malice against Bolsheviks is bitter and unending
Beaverbrook 'll claim the corpses were pretending!

EGLANTYNE JEBB

The *Manchester Guardian* yesterday published a review
of our fund's *Famine* film, and a very good one too,
by their cinematographic critic, C. A. Lejeune,
though her article shows a great deal more concern
for new films in full colour not like ours in monochrome,
nonetheless she grants that our images
(*Reads.*)   '*bring home
as words can never* (note that never!) *bring
the dread and the hopelessness of Volga suffering.*'
And this is from the *Daily Telegraph*, 20th Jan:
(*Reads.*) '*No film has shown such horror since cinema
    began.*'
The other films she writes about though must make ours
    much duller
as these are made with a process that shows things in
    full colour.
Every day they're developing more brilliant technique
like the colour cinematograph shown here just last
    week.

SHELDON

Any increase in reality surely must be good!
In the films of the future blood will look like blood.
Movie makers won't have their accustomed monochrome
    recourse,
when they want blood depicted, to Hershey's chocolate
    sauce.

EGLANTYNE JEBB

But to be honest I still think monochrome
might be the best medium to get our message home.
I think our film makes the Russians' desperate plight
look even more harrowing in plain old black and white.

SHELDON

Yes, pictures are getting better by the day.
We've had this modest movie made about the ARA.
It shows our American Relief Administration
working to rescue the Russians from starvation.
It concentrates less on horror more on gratitude displayed
by the starving of the Volga for US relief and aid.

RUTH FRY

I was in Samara when some of it was made.
Yes, I was in the region and saw it being 'shot'.
But can you call it reality? Unfortunately not!

SHELDON

Miss Fry! Whatever can you possibly mean?

RUTH FRY

I'm referring above all to one particular scene.
Your ARA 'movie', had control of it been mine
(and I'm not sure if you'll support me, Eglantyne),
there are certain aspects of it where I'd've drawn the line.
I saw the cameraman take a scoop of corn and throw
grains precious to the watchers in the melting snow.
The seed corn they'd seen him so casually scatter
was for them a literally life and death matter.
He then filmed the starving children (surely questionable
    taste)
feverishly searching so not one grain went to waste,
fossicking the slushy ice to fish up every grain,
and your man at his camera, when I ventured to complain,
simply shrugged and said to me, 'That's movies, honey.'

Sheldon laughs.

I confess I didn't find this observation funny.
Then with another shrug I watched him lean
back towards his lens and shoot exactly the same scene.
Then if he wanted peasants kissing food-relievers' feet
and didn't get the image and wanted a repeat

your cameraman discovered they co-operated more
if food supplies were doled out after not before.
Anyone who's had to live on dung and pounded roots
didn't see a problem in being asked to kiss your boots.
But you begin to suspect that something's less than true
when you see a starving peasant waiting for his cue
to kneel down at the feet of ARA relievers, then,
If his fawning wasn't fulsome, be forced to kneel again.
All I want to ask you is, do you believe this is the way
you'll promote what are the real achievements of the
    ARA?

SHELDON

Yes, they're real achievements, that no one can deny
though there are detractors (and the Bolsheviks!) who
    try.
They're the sort of achievements other agencies resent.
Let's remember the ARA contributes up to 91%
of all aid sent to Russia now in 1922.
And Miss Jebb, if I may make use of your machine,
I'd like to show us guys in action, life size, on the
    screen.
Not that I undervalue what both you ladies do.
Miss Jebb's *Save the Children*, and Quakers like Miss Fry
have supplied the other 10% we can't (as yet) supply.
And you, sir, Dr Nansen, the famine's leading light,
the beacon of benevolence beaming through the night.

RUTH FRY

The point I really feel I have to make
is, how is the suffering truthful when he has to stage
    his 'take'?
I only bring this up to show you can't rely
on film as truth, and that the camera can lie.
So perhaps Professor Murray's right that words can sway
more than so-called reality captured in this way.

EGLANTYNE JEBB
Professor Murray would prefer that moving pictures speak
(and even better I imagine if they spoke in ancient Greek!)
but sadly so far they've not perfected that technique.

GILBERT MURRAY
But I fear I find it, I might almost say, obscene
to have such shocking pictures projected on a screen.
But then I'm a fuddy-duddy and not at all *au fait*
with all the modern methods available today.

EGLANTYNE JEBB
But film is the direction our campaign should take.
Anything's worth trying for those little children's sake.
Does the means matter if, by shocking, we persuade
the otherwise reluctant to give cash to famine aid?

GILBERT MURRAY
Eglantyne, sorry. I simply can't agree.
For me the most persuasive means is always poetry.
(And I suspect your uncle Richard would think the same
    as me!)
A messenger who's thought about the things he's seen
and not an unmediated image thrown on to a screen,
shows a human mind and heart 's had time to brood
on the witnessed horror sometimes of such a magnitude
it's too overwhelming to take on, a monstrous theme
betrayed by any utterance less violent than a scream . . .
Sometimes you will see that a Greek poet puts in cries,
cries not in metre, like *pheu* or, more frequently, *ai-ai*s.
These are 'extrametrical' – that is, emotional signs
of the inexpressible anguish that generates the lines.
It's as if the messenger were allowed a sort of token
    scream
to show the level of the agony behind the measured
    theme.
The cries indicate the inarticulate degree

of suffering inexpressible outside of poetry.
I know I may appear a rather obsessive sort of bore
but it's this that poetry was invented for
to give focus to our suffering and to our pain
and the more it's done through language the more we'll
    stay humane.
Reliance on devices like the photograph and slide
will lead, I rather fear, to linguistic suicide.
We must keep on challenging language to engage
with all we suffer from in this new modern age.
If it doesn't have the words we must challenge it to find
new ones that will measure up to the disasters of mankind.
I think we fall into a deep defeatist trap
to regard poetry superseded by the slide show or the snap!
If it's to a modern appliance that you must go
I would sooner place my trust in the power of radio.
You know, I genuinely believe that I have often seen
vivider pictures on the wireless than the screen.

SYBIL THORNDIKE

I know you've told me, Gilbert, Greek tragedians could,
had they wished to, like us, use buckets of stage blood.
They weren't theatrically backward, so why didn't they?
I know you think it's because they'd found a better way.

GILBERT MURRAY

The messenger speech. A messenger speech
reaches depths in the heart mere pictures never reach.
If the messenger's on target, the mind's eye of the hearer
more than vision itself brings horror even nearer.

EGLANTYNE JEBB

Dr Nansen's photographs no Beaverbrook newshound
despite his devious efforts can possibly confound.

GILBERT MURRAY

The next time there are millions of starving mouths to feed
you'll need to boost the voltage to give the shock you need

to waken up the conscience, and the next time even more
shocking illustrations of a famine or of war.
You have to face it, most people hate to look
at horrors and will react like Beaverbrook.
Which is why I think that your campaign can reach
more people through persuasive (i.e. poetic) speech.

NANSEN

So, Dr Murray, are you only recommending verse
as a means of emptying a charitable purse?

RUTH FRY

Dr Murray, Miss Thorndike, don't you have a way
to enact a person dying in a dramatic play?

GILBERT MURRAY

Miss Thorndike can advise us, Sybil, can you not?

RUTH FRY

Yes, but I don't mean pretending to be shot
or stabbed, and fall down and hold the breath
and adopt the total immobility of death.
Supposing it's starvation an actor chose to play
he'd have to fast for months to get to look that way.
There is scarcely a gram of flesh beneath the skin.
It would take you months of fasting to look as thin
if you were to play the Hecuba of Buzuluk.

SYBIL THORNDIKE

But a portrayal involves far more than how I look!
The words, my empathy, the feelings of my heart
are far more important when I play a part.
All we need are the right lines and imagination
and even a well-fed actor can portray starvation.

SHELDON

Dancing's sure a no-no. I can tell you that.
Saw Isadora Duncan dance the famine. She was fat.
I know she's an artiste of huge worldwide esteem
but she took the Russian famine as her balletic theme.

No matter how much besotted ballet-buffs respect her
her present bulk's not suitable to dance a starving spectre.
She pranced about in skimpy silks to a Scriabin *étude*.
but didn't seem to me like one deprived of food.
In extreme times I doubt we need ballet or a play
but practical men like Nansen here and Hoover's ARA.
In the dire straits of famine there's not much call for
    dancing.
Better Hoovers's ARA and Dr Fridtjof Nansen!
If I may project it and you'd all take a seat.
our film proves theatricals are sort of obsolete.

NANSEN
(*to Gilbert Murray*)
Nor could your Hecuba, Miss Thorndike, begin to
    audition
to speak for millions in the throes of malnutrition.
I fear even your star actress scarcely qualifies
to be a starving woman despite her slender size.
Though eminently talented and divinely svelte,
Sybil's hardly starving.

SYBIL THORNDIKE
            But I'd know how she felt!
I don't see why an actress, even one that's overweight,
isn't up to imagining a starving woman's fate!

NANSEN
Dear lady, I'm sure your tragic talent's great,
but even you seem portly for such impersonation,
a woman on the Volga in the last days of starvation.

SYBIL THORNDIKE
I'm in absolute disagreement when you say
I couldn't be a starving woman in a tragic play.
Why not? Why not? If we have the imagination
why shouldn't we portray the suffering of starvation?
We can imagine *anything* if we only would.
'The greatest instrument of moral good,'

that's the imagination, said the poet Shelley.
An actress can play starvation belly or no belly.
If the actress is up to it, starvation won't defeat her.
Imagination is the key.

GILBERT MURRAY
And metre, Sybil, metre!

SHELDON
I guess the so-called acting might get a wee bit closer
if your thespian 's afflicted with *anorexia nervosa*.
It's reality, reality recorded on this reel,
not actors pretending things that they don't feel.

*Sheldon switches off light as if to begin projecting
his film.*

SYBIL THORNDIKE
Honestly! You fucking Yanks!

Sybil switches light back on.

What the fuck
does it matter how I, if I'm acting, fucking look?

GILBERT MURRAY
Sybil, you know that swearing's anathema to me.

SYBIL THORNDIKE
I'm out of your control now. Let me be!

*Sybil Thorndike moves angrily from 'campaign room'
to the table laid for supper. To audience:*

I happen to believe that the theatre permits
an actress to play hunger and still have fleshy tits.
The only thing an actress like me needs to do
is say on stage I'm starving and you'll believe it's true.
She says, 'This is the Volga', she says, 'I'm starving there,'
though she's obese of body and the boards she treads
    quite bare.

The collective imagination of the audience will summon
the freezing snows of Saratov, the starving woman.

SYBIL THORNDIKE
(*as starving Volga Woman*)

Forgive me! Forgive me! I'm so feeble and so weak
from lack of provender I can scarcely even speak.
The last food I was fortunate to feel on my poor tongue
was bread we're forced to make from ground twigs and
    horse-dung.
We give the last hay to the horses then wait till they
    excrete
droppings still studded with nutricious ears of wheat.
A piece of horse-dung bread. And that was days ago.
The insides of our hovels are filling up with snow
since we made them roofless as their thatches, being
    wheat,
were greedily dismantled and ground up for us to eat.
Colder and colder. We'll be brought down to our knees
once river transport's finished when the Volga starts to
    freeze.
Everybody forages. They're desperate. Desperate. So am I.
Without some miracle occuring all of us will die.
Desperate. Desperate for food. It didn't matter what.
Some people, me included, put their pets into the pot.
But couldn't go as far as I saw others do
putting human flesh into their ghastly stew.
Women in labour hope their babies are born dead
and so be spared the burden of more mouths to be fed.
Those who can contrive abortions and the feeble little
    foetus
becomes the grisly broth-base for most desperate corpse-
    eaters.
Some feel the Lord has blessed them if their children die
and their flesh ends up filling for their famished parents'
    pie.
The dead have been dug up. Anything like meat,

even grubbed up from the grave, seems good enough
    to eat.
Burials in any case have to be delayed
because the earth's like iron and frost defeats the spade.
The cold of the region means the corpse is slow to rot
so stays in fresh condition and can end up in the pot.
And for desperate people dying each day of starvation
piles of frozen corpses are a terrible temptation.
They have nothing. The frozen meat's piled high.
Their, our, my stark choice was turn cannibal or die.
So though it was deeply shocking it was no surprise
to see the monstrous mountains diminishing in size
as one by one survivors crept back at night and took
preferably a stranger's corpse by stealth back home to
    cook.
I resisted. I resisted, but in the end had to succumb
and first sucked what bits of flesh were left off a human
    thumb.

I'd seen three babushkas with a steaming cooking pot
and because food was scarce I wanted to know what
they'd managed to scavenge and had to go and look
and find out what they'd gathered that was suitable
    to cook.
From clouds over the cauldron I couldn't really tell
but my mouth began to water simply from the smell.
Through the steam and the shimmer of the cauldron's
    heat
I could see that it was crammed with human hands and
    feet.
Instead of throwing up as you might think I'd do
my mouth watered at the fragrance of their foetid stew.
So many flocked round the cauldron to see if they could
    steal
anything worth gobbling, thumb, big toe, boiled heel.
The crowd around the cauldron couldn't be controlled,

hands were scalded grabbing hands well-casseroled
and my own hand went dipping through the gristly scum
coming up scalded but clutching a cooked thumb.
That first taste was my downfall. Downfall it was not.
I wouldn't have survived this far without corpse-flesh in
    my pot.
I became a cannibal. A cannnibal. The scalded hand
I got from grabbing that first gobbet became a kind of
    brand.
But even if I'm branded no one should exclude
me from humanity because I've lived on human food.
But if you do not wish this disgrace to fall
not just on those who had no choice but on us all,
from the feeble heart beneath this shrivelled breast
I appeal to every one of you, you mothers of the West,
to come to Russia's aid, so that a mother need
not break such terrible taboos when desperate to feed
her children on straw-shreds she's scavenged out of shit
or hellish manflesh *shashlik* sizzling on the spit.
Help me, *pazhalsta*, help me, help my little boy,
we are both almost beyond it. *Spasibo, spasibo bolshoi.*

> *Sybil Thorndike looks hungrily at laden table.*
>   *She gobbles up food from the plates of the diners
> and stuffs it into her mouth, grabbing at anything
> edible, creating chaos on the table.*
>   *Nansen, Gilbert Murray, Sheldon, Eglantyne Jebb
> and Ruth Fry back off horrified.*
>   *Sybil Thorndike sinks behind table, throwing up.*
>   *She re-emerges wiping her mouth. Then suddenly
> throws up over the table.*
>   *Sybil Thorndike shouts angrily at ARA Man.*

                    SYBIL THORNDIKE
Sorry if I'm not *actually* starving.

> *Calms down. Then breaks the moment with:*

                                        I'm starving! I'd enjoy
a little champagne supper across at the Savoy.

   Sybil Thorndike sweeps out.
    Blackout.

Part Two

Enter the ghost of Hjalmar Johansen with the Greek tragic mask. He is laughing behind it.

GHOST OF HJALMAR JOHANSEN
(*parodying Gilbert Murray*)
And the mouth is always open.
                    Why? Because
I've cast it as a woman who gives blow jobs to the boss.

He takes the mask and mimes a blow job.

Did you see him flirting? He'll flirt wi' owt, and more
    than flirt,
he'll fuck, will Fridtjof Nansen, almost owt dressed in
    a skirt.
Owt! blonde, brunette, redhead, skinny, squat, fat,
spinsters, widows, wedded, owt 'll do that's got a twat.
The Viking twinkles and the blue-eyed Nordic gaze
were enough to loosen almost any lady's stays.
No better way to get a lady's legs to part
than by being famous for a compassionate heart.
And Fridtjof the hero who 'sends the starving succour'
preys on famine females, the fanny-mad old fucker!
I think this commitment to the so-called caring cause
means wheedling his way into caring ladies' drawers.
As far as cunt 's concerned he thinks Darwin decreed
that Natural Selection needed lakes of Nansen's seed.
His taste's very catholic from chubby 'un to t' skinny 'un,
cunt-hunting justified as 'quintessentially Darwinian'.
I'll be always at your back however much you think
you've finally escaped the one destoyed by demon drink.

Well, I wonder if the demon drink's a lesser demon
than hose-piping the female sex with Fridtjof Nansen
    semen!

Johansen picks up mask again.

Nay, you're no cock-sucker, you're the sort of starving
    mite
them dining do-gooders went on about all night.
It's the open gob of hunger, the eyes that stare,
looking for an angel to sweep down from the air,
but the only angel you'll see with those open eyes
is Death floating out of snow-filled Volga skies.

'ere, poor little bugger, have a bite to eat.
What do you fancy, Murray's veg or Nansen's meat?

Johansen mimes gagging with the mask.

What's that? Speak up. Or do you only speak
Professor Murray's poetic ancient Greek?
What's that?

Johansen bends ear to mouth of mask.

                    Can't chew. Can't swallow. Too weak.

*Johansen regards Sybil's pool of vomit. He smells it
to make sure.*

I know! I know! This stuff Sybil spewed up, that'll do.
It's sort of half-digested, good for invalids, this spew.
No. Don't want to? Tell you what. Me first and then you!

*Johansen spoons up some of Sybil's vomit, tastes
some, smacks his lips, then feeds the mask.*

Don't be disgusted. Once you're a ghost you'll spread
even still warm vomit like dripping on your bread.
Ghosts are no longer bound by human inhibition
and break all bounds of behaviour and nutrition.

*Johansen takes a knife and a slice of bread and spreads
a good dollop of vomit onto the bread. He takes a
bite out of it.*

Ugh? What do you mean: ugh! One day
you too'll guzzle on such gobbets like a ravenous gourmet.
You might throw up at present at the thought of summat
   spewed
being not for mopping up but for slurping up as food.
Be warned: a scoop of cold puke will seem a gourmet
   treat
in the coming days of glacial gloom with nothing left to
   eat.
The future frozen wastes 'll create an appetite
that would even stoop to lapping up a pool of runny shite.
There's human evolution. The triumphant of the species
foraging for nourishment in vomit and in faeces!

*Johansen makes to butter another slice. Then puts
down the knife. Looks at the mask.*

You'll all look like this poor bugger with his gob agape
gagging for grub in the final sunless famine with no
   escape.
Weigh up your chances. Will the vegetarian croak before
or after the less finickety flesh-wolfing carnivore?
You'll want a cuddle then, to be cradled as you die
without the energy to utter the weakest squeak or cry.

Johansen cradles mask.

When starvation rules the land, why is the food
that famine makes a mountain of, human flesh, tabooed?
They all find cannibalism barbarous. I don't see why.
In extremes like on the Volga you turn cannibal or die.
Only those starvation drove to break the last taboo
had the faintest hope in hell of ever coming through.
Nansen and I should know. We'd both of us be dead

if all we'd done was moan we'd got no wheat for bread.
We were gastronomically inventive out there at the Pole,
creative and not squeamish with all kinds of casserole,
anything, walrus, seal, fox, gull, guillemot,
we shot 'em when we saw 'em and popped 'em in the pot.
A human being's not, thank God, that poor restricted
    brute
the panda of China, only eating bamboo shoot,
and hasn't the survival skills to seek a substitute.
So why be shocked when famine makes men break
taboos formerly binding for survival's sake?
Even those items most tyrannically tabooed
seem in times of famine the most delicious food.
Even the sweetest dearest grandchild but recently defunct
can be the basis of the broth in which horse-dung bread
    gets dunked.
I think this Russian world of such terrible extremes
can hardly be survived on vegetarian regimes.
Poor Professor Gilbert Murray would be quite aghast
that not only meat, but people meat, is part of their
    repast.
Simple meat makes him protest, but he'd protest far
    louder
if he'd smelled the chunks of childflesh cooking in the
    chowder.

Better be a cannibal and live on human meat
than kill the horse you'll need to sow the coming season's
    wheat.
No harvest means more famine, but the question's how,
once they've eaten the horses, will they drag the heavy
    plough?
So full marks to the woman who bakes the undigested bits
that can be carefully salvaged from the droppings a
    horse shits.
I should've asked Dr Murray, Nansen's squeamish chum,

if hay's disqualified as veggie if it's been through a beast's
   bum.
Couldn't it count as veggie-fodder if the half-digested
   straw
has first passed through the bowels of a fellow herbivore?
Those who tried to keep the horses they didn't want to
   slay
used their survivor's instincts and made the precious hay
nourish both horse and owner in a most ingenious way.
The hay 's chewed by the horses. The starving folk can't
   wait
for the horse to digest its dinner and evacuate.
They have to guard the horses, though, in case somebody
   steals
the turds, the starving treasure for their own clandestine
   meals.
A horse fart's a fanfare that alerts shit-thieves to come
and gather the abundance cascaded from its bum.
Unlike Dr Nansen, the Darwinian in me 's fired
to hear of survival practices so poetically inspired.
The Nansen of the North Pole would certainly allow
the cannibal behaviour he seems to balk at now.
The League of Nations' Nansen, in his new soft-hearted
   role,
has silenced the Nansen that I knew at the Pole.
Now that he's embraced this international cause
he's cast aside commitment to old Darwinian laws,
helping bungling Bolsheviks, keeping them alive
when, by the rules of Darwin, there's no chance they'd
   survive.
Nansen of the North Pole, the Nansen that I knew,
would never let a loser jump Selection's fodder queue.
I'm still a Darwinian and for me when those who've died
will appear in public on Nansen's lantern slide
and be projected in the hushed shocked lecture hall

they'll reinforce the maxim that the weak go to the wall.
I bet these starving Bolsheviks felt so blessed in their fate
being visual blackmail for the Western overweight.

Blackout.
As for Nansen's lecture to the various cities in Part
One, screens are flown in until there are three lantern-
slide screens.
Nansen is in front of a lantern-slide screen again.

NANSEN

I came to London twenty-five years ago.
The slides I showed you then were of Arctic ice and snow.
Those years ago I told you that the most uplifting sights
that I had ever witnessed were the Polar Northern Lights.
Now, I fear, it's my duty to put up on this screen
the most horrific pictures I believe you've ever seen.
And I should in fairness warn you that every lantern slide
I'm going to show you will make you horrified.
I who painted the Aurora and its shimmering swathes
	of light
now must show you Russian horrors in bleaker black
	and white.
Once again the landscape is endless ice and snow
but Famine stalks the Volga, laying millions low,
like the poor unfortunates I am about to show.

First slide.
Nansen begins his lecture tour of Britain.

NANSEN
(*before the second screen*)
I came to Newcastle twenty-five years ago.
The slides I showed you then were of Arctic ice and snow.
Now, I fear, I have to put up on the screen
the most horrific pictures I believe you've ever seen.
Famine stalks the Volga, laying millions low,
like the poor unfortunates I am about to show.

Second slide.

NANSEN
(before the third screen)
I came to Aberdeen twenty-five years ago.
The slides I showed you then were of Arctic ice and snow.
Now, I fear, I have to put up on the screen
the most horrific pictures I believe you've ever seen.
Famine stalks the Volga, laying millions low,
like the poor unfortunates I am about to show.

> *Third slide.*
> *Then a sequence of terrifying slides from the*
> *Russian famine appears simultaneously on all three*
> *screens, ending with one of two naked corpses on the*
> *three screens, so that in all there are six.*

A brother and a sister on this, my final slide,
to comfort one another held hands as they died.
I leave you this last image to linger in your mind,
two starved siblings, their stiff fingers intertwined.
If all of you here tonight could spare a small donation
we could begin to put a stop to such obscene starvation.

> *Exit Nansen.*
> *Enter Hjalmar Johansen, looking at the three*
> *screens and the corpses displayed on them.*

JOHANSEN
God, you could see that this emaciated bunch
weren't on the guest list at Nansen's 'famine lunch'.
These famine freak-show specimens with shrunken,
    frozen tits
haven't taken light refreshment at the local fucking Ritz.
Did you see them stuff their faces, did you see them
    cramming
cakes into their crumb-flecked gobs to aid the Volga
    famine?

They'd go through the motions of empathetic grief
moued between mouthfuls of tenderly done beef.
Maybe for a moment your fate will make them pause
in mashing more moist morsels in their masticating jaws.

Once you've donned some vestments and been vetted for
    disease
you'd be cordially welcomed to a little wine and cheese.
Best veil your rock-hard titties and your icicle-hung muff,
Aberdeen's a wee bit backward at buffets in the buff.
There'll be lots left for us! If you could escape out of
    the slide
you could wolf the surplus and be richly satisfied.
Be resurrected by your hunger, burst out through the
    screen!
Sink your teeth into the turkey, slurp the soup from the
    tureen.
Don't let it go to waste, eat up, and while you dine
I'll sit down and toast you with what's left of the wine.

Johansen picks up Nansen's pointer.

These corpses are going to make a *corps de ballet* –
if you want to dance the famine, go on, musicians, play.
Get those strings whining, play that pulsing beat
and try to get these corpses to leap up to their feet.
Just get the bloody Bolshoi bowing those violins
and they'll jump up and shake their cash-collecting tins.

Come on, shake a leg, we need to see you rise
and dance Isadora's *Famine* before our very eyes . . .
They don't want their weak hearts torn or their spirits
    rending.
Rise up and dance and show us it's pretending.
You're really only actors who've lost a lot of weight
to portray with more perfection starvation's sorry state.
They must have searched worldwide in the audition
to find such perfect matches for extremest malnutrition.

To starved corpses on the screen:

You owe your benefactors a celebratory ballet
to show a spark of gratitude to Hoover's ARA.
Or why not honour, I know, Nansen the explorer
by dancing the joyful ballet the *Aurora*,
composed, played and danced by your lucky Russian kin
who left with Nansen passports the country you're
    stuck in.

A lush musical flourish from the Aurora *ballet.*
    Nothing moves on the slides. Johansen demonstrates
    the futility of the exercise.

They'll stay behind the borders of the screen or slide
yearning for a passport to the warmer world outside.

He goads the corpses on the screen.

I know what I'll do. I'll do summat daft
and make these corpses corpse, and once they've laughed
you'll know that they're actors pretending to be dead
and you can worry about what's really real instead.
It won't take much to prove they're just a fake.
When I fart just watch their bony midriffs shake.

He farts. Nothing.

Go on, do some little movement just to show
you're not really dead, like wiggle your big toe.
Go on, you had us fooled. We're mightily impressed
by the thespian corpses. Bravo. Now get dressed.
Each of you have chosen a convincing corpse-like pose
and we applaud your stillness, now put on your clothes.
Move! Make a movement! Let them off the hook.
Show you're alive to them at least and I won't look.

Johansen covers his eyes. Nothing.

Did they move? No? Bad luck, Beaverbrook!

So, you see, they're genuinely dead and nothing's fake
though I wish it all had been for everybody's sake.
I'll leave these to immigrate into your imagination
and escape the confines of photographed starvation.
I'll leave you to try to rouse them, and let you lot try
    to coax
them into dancing, or to corpse at your daft jokes.
Try it all together.

   Johansen begins to go then stops.

           If they're real or just pretend
isn't probably important in the end.

   Exit Johansen, passing on the mask to Nansen.
     A long silence, then a hum begins and grows.
   Then on all three screens simultaneously the corpses
   suddenly sit up and scream.
     The screams develop and re-echo and multiply.
     Nansen and Gilbert Murray listen to the screams
   under the UN logo.

NANSEN

Listen, listen, all these multiplying shrieks
which started at the Volga turn into screaming Greeks.
I thought my spirit, like the *Fram*, could not be sunk
till it multiplied to millions the *Scream* of Edvard Munch.

GILBERT MURRAY

I'm convinced now that Greek tragedy had screams
to show the poetry that followed dealt with great
    extremes.
What irked me as not metrical I know now plays a part
in priming the emotion of the poetic art.
Classicists, myself included, haven't given enough note
to shrieks that are strong enough to scorch the shrieker's
    throat.
When translators give us the inadequate 'Oh woe!'

it's because they didn't know what I now know
that those cries outside the metre the *ai-ai* and the *pheu*
were really intended as an actor's screaming cue,
an occasion outside poetry where the actor could let go,
a scream from the heart that broke the metric flow,
not to be pathetically translated into English as 'Oh woe!'

NANSEN

I rather think that the twentieth-century Muse
has restricted her vocabulary to those *ai-ai*'s and *pheu*s
Sorry to cut you short, Murray, I meant murdered Greeks,
real people and not actors, were uttering those shrieks.
Greeks murdered by the Turks along the Smyrna quays
now in 1922, Professor, not in Euripides.
After so many millennia your Hellenism dies
in Asia Minor with increasing screams and cries.
A migration of this magnitude has not been known
    before
the Greeks were defeated in the Greco-Turkish War.
Already overcrowded vessels, hunger and disease
have killed off 300,000 of the desperate refugees.

I spoke to Johansen in my mind: 'This is one for you,'
I said. 'The Opera House in Athens in 1922!
Like you grinding down my crayons to caulk our kayak
    leaks –
posh opera boxes housing homeless Asia Minor Greeks!
You'd be glad to turn over that velvet plush, to them
not posh perfumed parties applauding *La Bohème*.
Tiers crammed with Greeks made homeless by the Turks
and not come to clap their hands at one of Mozart's
    works.
Each box a curtained flatlet across which washing's hung
instead of those in scent and furs at *Götterdämmerung*.
He'd say: 'Shut up, Dr Murray, homeless people need a
place to eat and sleep and shit, not bloody old *Aida*!'

GILBERT MURRAY

It's as if this theatre here in London, the Olivier,
instead of being full of people listening to my play,
through some disaster had been compelled to cram
this theatre with refugees, not people watching *Fram*.

NANSEN

Even that, to you, most sacred space of all,
the Theatre of Dionysus, crammed from wall to wall.
Imagine your *Trojan Women* chorus 10,000 times the size
not uttering great poetry but anguished screams and cries.
Murray, I hate to tell you, but you would despair
seeing bivouacs where Hecuba had her premiere.
Bivouacs of rags and branches, an open cooking fire
in the orchestra where Aeschylus first gave his *Oresteia*.
The theatre of Aeschylus, Sophocles, Euripides
now housing hundreds of Asia Minor refugees.
The world's wailing and screaming's going to increase
infinitely greater than the grief of ancient Greece.

> *Nansen gets out the marble tragic mask presented to*
> *him by Gilbert Murray and Sybil Thorndike.*

Civilisation as we know it seems destined to collapse
and the tragic masks of Europe will only shut their traps.
Future disasters, future famines, future wars
will slowly close and silence those once always-open jaws.
In the dramas of the future there'll only come
some final means of mourning in a simple sombre hum.
If we can't hope for solutions from our precious League,
what good 's your Greek drama –

> *Nansen gives the tragic mask back to Gilbert Murray.*
> *Exit Gilbert Murray, looking at the mask.*
> *Nansen alone.*

                              – what good my Edvard Grieg?
My spirit longs to fly into the silent sky

untroubled by the screaming the Earth is anguished by.
Above the flight of birds to peer from the Zeppelin
at the wilderness of ice I was my happiest in.
And maybe imagine I see far, far down below
the hut where we wintered buried long ago,
the hut long ago entombed where Johansen and I
learned, despite our difference, to embrace or die.

*Nansen walks thoughtfully to the spot where his
armchair and phonogram were previously placed. He
hears the scratchy Grieg song sung by Eva. It turns into
screams, and from the three phonograms projected on
the shutters comes a 'pure' version of the song towards
which Nansen walks.*

*The projected phonograms change into an endless
Arctic landscape. The Grieg song becomes a huge
orchestral version, enveloping Nansen in his death.*

*A South Bank panorama fades up through the
endless Arctic waste.*

*The NT is reflected in the Thames. The reflection
breaks up.*

*Contemplating the tragic mask, Gilbert Murray waits
outside the National Theatre for Sybil Thorndike,
who enters as if from crossing Waterloo Bridge from
the Savoy. Sybil puts her hands over Gilbert's eyes.*

GILBERT MURRAY
Sybil, is that alcoholic liquor I smell on your breath?

SYBIL THORNDIKE
The champagne was heaven after thirty years of death.
And would you believe it, the Savoy's old *maitre d'*
despite my long absence keeps my table free?
Life! Oysters and champagne at the Savoy!

GILBERT MURRAY
Neither of those items are ones that I'd enjoy!

SYBIL THORNDIKE
Dr Nansen would have bought me some champagne.

GILBERT MURRAY
My hero had some qualities I cannot entertain.

SYBIL THORNDIKE
I just wanted a bit of gladness, life and light
before more oblivion in the Abbey's Arctic night.

Sulky silence.

GILBERT MURRAY
Maybe all my belief in tragedy 's an academic sham.
But I believed in tragedy like Nansen in his *Fram*,
a vessel of the spirit that could withstand the force
of crushing coldness and still move on its course.

What does it amount to, the story that we've told,
the struggle against the ice and men's hearts just as cold?
Not being aware that he was, in fact, a dying man
Nansen published the proposal of his 'AeroArctic' plan
in January 1930. He was going to use
the airship the *Graf Zeppelin* in the first Arctic
    stratocruise.
But by May of the same year my explorer friend was dead,
dying with his North Pole plans still buzzing in his head.
They say that 'AeroArctic' was the last word that he said.
He died on his fjord-side verandah in his chair
whispering 'AeroArctic' and floating through the air
to go the 'farthest north' men can. Neither he nor I
believe there's anywhere to go to when we die
but he sometimes used to say that if there was a soul
and it went anywhere it would be like the Pole.

SYBIL THORNDIKE
The grave's pretty perishing I'd have to agree.
What does anyone amount to? You? Me?

All our performances? Our writings? All for what?
A bright stage, then a blackout without a follow spot.
You and I did our bit for the ailing League of Nations.
The memory of my Hecuba in your great translation 's
the deepest I retain. One of my, I mean *our*, hits.

GILBERT MURRAY

Yes, but its set, those Doric columns, was bombed flat in
    the Blitz.
What after all did our *Trojan Women* do
to help the League to spare us World War Two?
It did as much as it had already done
when it went to America in World War One.
Absolutely nothing! Nothing! It played the USA
when Britain was losing a thousand men a day.
All those what Eliot brands 'Swinburnian' verse
    translations
couldn't hope to save the floundering League of Nations.
Aeschylus trucked out corpses on the ekkyklema.
We've seen the world one corpse-piled ekkyklema,
the corpses of Auschwitz, Dresden, Hiroshima.
A German said, and I'm beginning to agree,
the horrors of Auschwitz silenced poetry.

He looks at the river.

When we reach the Abbey, we'll be separated soon,
let's take a last look at the river shimmering in the moon,
and at the National Theatre. Did you know
Nansen predicts a globe entirely ice and snow?
A world, when the sun cools, a world that will be free
of Evolution's greatest failure, us, Humanity.

SYBIL THORNDIKE

How could I not know? He tried that one on me
as well as all his repertoire of English poetry:
especially, 'Had we but world enough and time,

this coyness, my dear Sybil, were no crime.'
I believe his final Ice Age theory may be another ploy
Nansen may make use of when he finds the ladies coy.
Have you yourself acquired one survival skill?

GILBERT MURRAY

Tragedy was my *Fram*. I couldn't hunt or kill.
In Mittagong, New South Wales, as a boy I got the hang
of throwing and recatching the Abo boomerang.

SYBIL THORNDIKE
(*laughs*)

To be truthful I can't begin to picture you,
of all people, Gilbert, boomeranging kangaroo!

GILBERT MURRAY

But just imagine it, the ice!

SYBIL THORNDIKE
Gilbert, I'd rather not.

If I imagine the world's end, I'd prefer it hot.

GILBERT MURRAY

But if Nansen's prediction one day does come true
imagine how it's going to look round here in Waterloo.
Icebergs round the Abbey, maybe Big Ben poking through.
Our Abbey, Parliament, the NT, all below
the everlasting tombstone of Nansen's ice and snow.
A few flags on the tops of buildings might protrude
like that one Nansen planted at his northern latitude.
I fear that my principles won't let me wear furs
as Nansen says we must do when that sad end occurs.

SYBIL THORNDIKE

He offered me a stole of a silver fox he'd shot
and cooked the spine of in his Arctic cooking pot
'I'll offer you,' he said, 'this stole made from my silver fox
to grace your slender neck and shoulders in your opera
    box.

Look at its tiny teeth. When you wear it, think of mine
sucking and nibbling the best bits off its spine.'

GILBERT MURRAY

How horrible! How horrible!

SYBIL THORNDIKE

                    It was beautiful, the stole.
In exchange he wanted something he was 'starved of at
   the Pole'.

GILBERT MURRAY

Whatever could he mean?

SYBIL THORNDIKE

                I imagine that he means
like you he got frustrated when he couldn't get his greens.

GILBERT MURRAY

So he had a vegetarian streak and I had no idea!

SYBIL THORNDIKE

I suppose he must have pined for sprouts as a Polar
   pioneer!
He had company, of course, but is Johansen who you'd
   choose
to share one's personal passion for the poetic Muse?

GILBERT MURRAY

Nansen and Johansen, even their names rhyme
though they seemed at daggers drawn almost all the time.
They seemed like total opposites, chalk and cheese,
a sort of Arctic Dr Faust and Mephistopheles.

I forgot to ask you, did it please you, the NT?
I'm not entirely certain it's the proper place for me.
No matter how brilliant you are when you translate –

SYBIL THORNDIKE

And you *are* brilliant, Gilbert!

GILBERT MURRAY
                              – all translations date.
I don't for a minute imagine that I dare aspire
to a National Theatre revival of my *Oresteia*.
I'm more than disgruntled to see they only use
bloody Yorkshire roughnecks like Harrison and Hughes.

SYBIL THORNDIKE
In all the years I've known you I've never heard you swear.

GILBERT MURRAY
I'd swear at T. S. Eliot. You know he's with us over there?

SYBIL THORNDIKE
I did, but we haven't spoken.

GILBERT MURRAY
                              Tosser T.S.E.,
with a memorial in the Abbey seventy feet from me!

SYBIL THORNDIKE
How cosy for you both! You must show me where,
and I'll visit. I did a play of his.

GILBERT MURRAY
(*tetchy*)
                              I'm only too aware.
It stuck in my craw and, frankly, it still sticks
that you did Eliot's *Family Reunion* in 1956.
Your betrayal killed me in the May of the next year.

SYBIL THORNDIKE
You were over ninety – don't be tetchy, Gilbert dear.

They enter the Abbey. They hear a hum.

SYBIL THORNDIKE
Whatever's that? Too late to be the choir!

The hum grows louder and more threatening.

FRAM

GILBERT MURRAY
It sounds like the Furies from the *Oresteia.*

*Gilbert Murray and Sybil Thorndike move through the
Abbey. Gilbert puts the mask back on the monument.
Then in the air and on the ground are the coloured
reflections from the stained glass of the Rose Window.*

SYBIL THORNDIKE
What's that beautiful light, like an Aurora in the air?

GILBERT MURRAY
The moon through the stained glass Aeschylus.

SYBIL THORNDIKE
                                 Aeschylus? Up there?
A pagan in the Abbey window. Gilbert, show me where.

GILBERT MURRAY
In the rose's right hand quarter, starting centre, count
one, two, and three is Aeschylus, Greek tragedy's great
    fount.
He's the spirit in my life I most often seem to summon.

SYBIL THORNDIKE
He shares his petal of the rose with the only woman
in the entire circle as far as I can see.
To the right of Aeschylus. Gilbert, who is she?
Who's the woman on his left whose presence seems
    to blaze
through the Abbey in these auroral rays?
It's the red light from her garment that I'm seeing shed
by the moon in the air above me, on my face, my head.

GILBERT MURRAY
You won't believe this, Sybil, it's the Sibyl.

SYBIL THORNDIKE
                         Me?

GILBERT MURRAY

You're the only Sybil who deserves the prefix THE!

SYBIL THORNDIKE

How gallant you are, Gilbert! But she's beautiful, and look,
in her left hand, she's clutching her prophetic book.
I wonder if like Fridtjof Nansen the Sibyl can foresee
the freezing of our planet and the end of history.

GILBERT MURRAY

I've been less keen on the Sibyl, and I know you'll understand,
since you-know-who used her in his 'poem' *The Waste Land*!
And this is Poets' Corner. All those poets who served the Muse.
But don't look or stop at that one! It's you-know-who's!

They start going past Eliot's memorial, and Murray can't resist stopping.

GILBERT MURRAY

I lived past ninety years without alcohol or meat
nor ever used language a prof should not repeat.
I want to swear at Eliot but don't want to be overheard
by any of the bishops if I use a naughty word.

SYBIL THORNDIKE

Go on, Gilbert, let all that grievance out.
and if you feel the urge to, go ahead and shout.

Gilbert Murray stamps on T. S. Eliot's memorial and his shouting creates Abbey echoes.

GILBERT MURRAY

Eliot, you fucking desiccated cat-exploiting Yank!
It's a pity that you ever left your day job at the bank.
How was that?

SYBIL THORNDIKE
Bravo, Gilbert, that's the spirit, swear!

GILBERT MURRAY
There are so many names I want to call him but don't
dare.

Murray stamps on Eliot's memorial.

SYBIL THORNDIKE
You told me not to stop or look but you just can't resist.
If I didn't know you were teetotal I'd say that you were
pissed.

GILBERT MURRAY
Not, as you say, inebriated but stupidly in thrall
to the kind of petty grievances that sometimes dog us all.
Not . . . intoxicated, no! I'm still steadfastly TT.

SYBIL THORNDIKE
Sadly, as I've noticed, when you're dead you have to be.

GILBERT MURRAY
I promised to take you to see where Larry's laid
then we must part company, dear Sybil, I'm afraid.

*Gilbert Murray and Sybil Thorndike move through
the Abbey and stand over the chiselled plaque under
which the ashes of Laurence Olivier lie.*

SYBIL THORNDIKE
One by one we go. There can't be many left alive.
I was his Jocasta in 1945.

GILBERT MURRAY
(*tetchy*)
Mmm, the *Oedipus* 'translated' by W. B. Yeats!
Doesn't know a word of Greek yet he still 'translates'!
They all do it now. I doubt if any poets speak
the language they 'translate' from and most certainly not
Greek.

SYBIL THORNDIKE

He was Coriolanus. I was Volumnia, his mum.

The continuing hum comes nearer and nearer.

What or who do you suppose it is, that eerie hum?

GILBERT MURRAY

Who's there? Who's there? I thought we were alone.

The hum continues.

Who's there? Are you a ghost that makes that mournful moan?

Enter a Kurdish Poet with a sewn mouth. The Poet wears a placard round his neck that says KURDISH POET SEEKS UK CORNER. *His eyes and ears are also sewn together.*

Oh God! Who did that to you, poor fellow?

Poet with Sewn Mouth points to self.

GILBERT MURRAY

You?

Well, that's a pretty rum thing for you to do.

To Sybil Thorndike:

How bizarre of the man, indeed how crude, to choose
to come like this, mutilated, to the sanctum of the Muse.
This figure with a sewn-up mouth, this poet, this Kurd,
violates this sacred place where great poets are interred.
With these festering mutilations it seems to me
Poets' Corner is the last place this poor man should be.

Addresses Poet with Sewn Mouth:

Not place! No! Over river! St Thomas's, A&E!

GILBERT MURRAY

Goodbye, Sybil, I'd've written better if I could.

SYBIL THORNDIKE

Goodbye, Gilbert! Yes, I know you would.
Wear your laurels, Gilbert.

GILBERT MURRAY
                    I don't think I ought.
I think my poetic efforts have rather fallen short.
I don't deserve them. Besides, I couldn't wear a wreath
that T. S. Eliot's been lying underneath.
I still hear T. S. Eliot –

SYBIL THORNDIKE
                    Oh Gilbert, my poor darling!

GILBERT MURRAY
– stuck in his critic's rictus, superciliously snarling.
On my final exit now all that I'll be hearing
's not audience applause but Eliot still sneering!
My farewell couplet's the very last time
you'll ever hear a terrible Gilbert Murray rhyme.
Farewell, Sybil. Oh woe! I feel a futile failure,
a disgrace to the Muses, to Oxford, to Australia!

*Gilbert Murray stares at the tragic mask, then smashes
it, then screams. The screams echo round the Abbey,
passing overhead above the theatre. Exit Gilbert.*

*The Kurdish Poet listens to the echoing scream and
the hum.*

*A red light from the sybil in the Rose Window falls
on Kurdish Poet.*

*Poet with Sewn Mouth hears the hum of a jumbo
overhead. He listens.*

*Sybil Thorndike listens to the hum of the aeroplane
getting louder and passing overhead above the theatre.*

SYBIL THORNDIKE

And what would you have written if you'd been asked
   to write

a play like poor old Gilbert tried to write tonight?

Sybil moves closer to the Poet.

You're the opposite of Gilbert's mask with sewn up
   mouth and eyes,
but I sense you're seeing something up there in the skies.
Jihadis in the cockpit? Or just a stowaway
trying to enter Britain in a jumbo jet wheelbay?

Plane hum.

Listen! Above the theatre, the hum of a big plane,
from the East or Africa, Conakry, Accra, Bahrain,
following the Thames flight path up to Heathrow,
the river, and the theatres on either side below.
Someone in a window seat wakes up and he can see
down below in London the Thames and the NT.
And maybe, cold and rigid in the dark wheelbay,
about to drop on London, an illegal stowaway.
Listen! Listen! Listen! The great jumbo hum
like the *basso profundo* of some huge harmonium.
If the wheelbay opened now you might look up and see
a corpse crash through the flytower into the NT.
Imagine how it took off, this particular humming plane,
this, let's say, a BA Boeing people boarded in Bahrain.
and the wheels have just retracted in the climbing DC10
and inside the wheelbay with no heat or oxygen,
the stowaway, at that height in the ascending jet,
is fearfully frightened but not quite frozen yet,
a stowaway in total darkness who still dares to think,
as proper cabin passengers are plied with their first drink
and chew their peanuts, still dares to think beneath,
the shivering stowaway with accelerating teeth,
still dares to think (but not for long) that there's a chance
he'll make it to Germany, the Netherlands or France,
or even here to London maybe now tonight,

frozen to death by passage through the Arctic cruising
    height.
This immigrant Icarus who stowed away and flew
was frozen in the wheelbay, and fell on a B&Q.
The thudding thwack of impact headfirst from the sky
on to the concrete car park of a mega-DIY.

In the voice of a B&Q cashier:

I'm a B&Q cashier. I clocked on at seven am
and passed the splattered brains and briefly glanced
    at them,
only glanced at them, and the feller, then disgustedly
    dismissed
it as some spew-spattered person more than pretty
    pissed.
I think most of us now would make that same
    assumption
that someone had OD'd on their alcohol consumption,
and was sleeping in his vomit. Not the rarest sight
in car parks over Britain after Saturday night.
I just mistook him (OK, I know you think I'm thick)
for one sleeping off his stupor, his face in his own sick.
I did think for a second, they don't go on the piss,
the Pakistanis, and collapse in puke like this.
Then I thought maybe the reason he came to the UK 's
to learn and conform to traditional British ways.
So I didn't notice that the vomit was the poor man's
    brains.

Sybil Thorndike stops being B&Q cashier.

So many would-be immigrants fall plunging out of planes.
Imagine such migrants falling onto Regent Street
like the raining men in bowlers in that painting of
    Magritte.
Death grants his 'Nansen passports' to every émigré

attempting to reach Europe as an airbus stowaway.
The airbus's belly opens, the crowd below it gawps
as a BA jumbo wheelbay gives birth to a stiff corpse.
And the wheelbay opens, the wheelbay opens wide
and disgorges the stowaway frozen stiff inside.
Such frozen corpses tumble out of jumbos in the sky
and thud on to an England they won't be welcomed by.
Dawn's almost here. Now the Sibyl's shed
her red anointing light on this poor poet's head.
With this abandoned laurel wreath this poet must be
    crowned
before sunrise drives me back again into the cold ground.

> *Sybil Thorndike takes a laurel wreath that we saw*
> *Gilbert Murray try on earlier and places it on the*
> *Kurdish Poet's head.*
> > *There is the deep hum of a jumbo overhead.*

SYBIL THORNDIKE

Sing the future like the Sibyl. Sing of what's to come.
If it can communicate, your mutilated hum.

> *She makes to leave.*

We, all the Abbey represents. It's had its day.
Wear the laurel wreath. Make poems. Make a play.

> *Sybil Thorndike stands at her memorial.*

And if you do, please, write a part for me.
Nothing too big. Anything. I'm always free.

> *Exit Sybil Thorndike into her memorial.*
> > *The Kurdish Poet becomes flooded with the red*
> *light from the window.*
> > *The Poet looks up and remains motionless, listening*
> *to the hum.*
> > *He hums also. His hum is envisioning the end of the*
> *world.*
> > *Ice appears on the floor of the Abbey.*

FRAM

At the climax of the Kurdish Poet's aria, the stained glass of the two Rose Windows shatters and falls in pieces on the ice like a broken Aurora.

There is the sound of creaking pack ice.

Icebergs burst through the floor of the Abbey.

Another hum begins, like a great swarm of bluebottles mixed with the aeroplane hum and the hum of the Kurdish Poet.

The humming continues. The Arctic wilderness returns, except that now it is Nansen's predicted future icy end of the world.

There is a totally iced-over Fram.

Into this landscape come two African Boys apparently dressed like Polar explorers, but in fact robed in millions of bluebottles who are making the hum we hear.

Enter Nansen.

NANSEN

You'll see now by the landscape spread in front of you
my prediction, experts have been happy to pooh-pooh,
that the world would end in ice has finally come true.
I had the same disbelief expressed by 'experts' when
  I crossed
Greenland the so-called 'wrong way' and not a man
  was lost,
or when I had the *Fram* built to survive the Arctic ice,
so you'd think that, after scoffing then being proved
  wrong twice,
your contemporaries might have heeded my cooling
  sun advice.
But no! They kept on insisting the opposite was true
till the seas started freezing over and then they knew.

While you are still able to listen and keep warm
the ghost of Fridtjof Nansen has a duty to perform.

These boys have been my inspiration, also my despair,
for their doomed expedition to the Arctic of the air.

To Boys:

For conquering the Aeroarctic in international space
take this flag I used to serve and plant it in this place,
to show, though nobody will see it, that you claim
what you have conquered in no single nation's name.

> *Nansen gives the two African Boys a flag on a stick*
> *which they plant into the icy stage, It is the UN flag*
> *with the world in white surrounded by the olive wreath.*

Let it fly, and flap. Though now it won't be seen
there will be ghosts like us remember what the emblems
  mean.
It suits this place. It could have been designed
as the emblem of the iced globe of now doomed
  humankind.
A world past all redemption where no one needs to mark
boundaries round nations all frozen in the dark.
To bring it properly up to date, though, the sea's blue
should also be depicted in icy white-out too,
to reveal the globe's surrender to those superior forces
that keep the orbits going and the planets in their courses,
forces with no hearts or empathy and no scrap of concern
whether in the end our Earth would freeze or burn.

> *Enter Ghost of Hjalmar Johansen.*

NANSEN
Johansen, come here, my friend.

JOHANSEN
                   I know, you told me so.

NANSEN
Hardly time for boasting. I promise not to crow.

JOHANSEN

And yon's the perfect flag to flap at the frozen Pole
of the icy darkness of the snuffed-out hopeful soul.

NANSEN

Did your ashes in their urn like mine identify
with these two young explorers of the Arctic sky?

JOHANSEN

Yes, when I realised they were doomed to die!

NANSEN

The blizzard of my ashes about to blow my bone-urn lid 's
brewing to a fury at the fate of these black kids.
who braved the Aeroarctic of the upper atmosphere
not in bear-fur sleeping bags but flimsy cotton gear.
Explorers, brave ones, with 'no line of retreat',
but with no preparation for what they'd wear or eat.
They were brave explorers but they did not prepare
except for one choc bar they'd clearly planned to share
if they felt peckish once they'd got into the air.
It was found all runny in one boy's rotting hand.
It reset and it remelted as they flew from land to land,
Finally in Africa a sticky choccy glove
rested on the shoulder of the friend he seemed to love.
What they really needed, brave explorers though they
    were,
was a pound of pemmican and a sleeping bag of fur.
They had all of Nansen's bravery with 'no line of retreat'
but didn't prepare like Nansen would for 30,000 ft.
How did they think they could possibly survive
when the Aeroarctic temperature is minus 45?
They entered the Aeroarctic in the sort of cotton gear
worn south of the Equator, where it's very hot all year.
Cotton shirts and shorts, car-tyre flip-flops on their feet –
casual and comfy wear for Guinea's baking heat
but fatally flimsy at 30,000 ft.

In their T-shirts, shorts and flip-flops they didn't prepare
for their pioneering journey to the Arctic of the air.
Just reach Europe, these frozen children thought,
and we'd be warmly welcomed, housed, clothed, taught.
They were frozen, frozen to death, in a DC10 wheelbay,
two adventurous children who naively stowed away.
Think of what could be made of that naive enterprise
and bravery, wasted in that wheelbay in the skies.

The Aeroarctic at the cruising height of jets
gets just as freezing as the North Pole ever gets.
It's as if they'd concentrated all our endless Arctic night
into that dark wheelbay in one seven hour flight.
Those boys didn't have a double bear-fur sack
like we who braved those temperatures and managed to
    get back.
They were a pair of friends, these two desperate refugees,
and a couple can cuddle as the air begins to freeze.
They had to lose their inhibitions, not be shy
of embracing one another to survive the freezing sky.
And they died intertwined, each boy wrapped round his
    friend,
so don't fall from the wheelbay when the wheels descend.
And don't splatter blood on the *Musée des Beaux Arts*
which houses Brueghel's Icarus who also fell as far.
Unlike an AeroArctic Icarus, who freezes and then falls,
their brains aren't aerosolled all over Brussels walls.
No one at *Sabena* knew their bodies were on board.
They left Brussels then flew back. Their bodies froze
    and thawed.
Their embracing corpses at cruising height refroze
and then, landing in hot Conakry, start to decompose.
Freeze/decompose, freeze/decompose on ten successive
    trips
till ground staff in Africa noticed foetid drips
of foul liquid and the dreadful acrid smell

of decomposition from the undercarriage well,
and foul puddles of putrescence on the ground,
and the wheelbay throbbing with a sombre buzzing sound
was probed and prodded and the rotting children found,
in an embrace where each boy seemed to enfold
the other in his arms against the gnawing cold,
the right knee of one between his friend's two thighs.
Like Polar explorers.

Nansen turns to Johansen.

> JOHANSEN
> Garbed not in furs but flies.
Each one garbed and breeked and hooded by a black
flocking, buzzing, feasting, heaving anorak.
Windblown pelts bespoke from a loud bluebottle swarm
as if they were explorers' furs that kept their corpses
> warm.
That double bag of ours might well have got them through
those regions of sub-zero the *Sabena* airbus flew.

> NANSEN
Our bear-fur bag and cuddling might have got them
> through,
As I embraced you, Hjalmar . . .

> JOHANSEN
> Sir, I cuddled close to you.

> NANSEN
We had nothing in common,

> JOHANSEN
> but we shared our human heat,

> NANSEN
and that was what they needed at 30,000 ft.

> JOHANSEN
We detested one another,

NANSEN

but nonetheless embraced
and survived sub-zero darkness in that Arctic waste.
We shared our warmth despite the hostility we felt,
despite being incompatible,

JOHANSEN

despite the way we smelt,
If we hadn't cuddled close there's no doubt that we'd've
    died,
but embracing

NANSEN

saved the idealist

JOHANSEN

and (for a time) the suicide.

NANSEN

And might help,

JOHANSEN

for a time,

NANSEN

when the cooled sun

makes reluctant cuddlers,

JOHANSEN
cuddlers,

NANSEN

out of everyone.

They put up the Fram *masts and rigging. The iced* Fram
*turns and moves away into the wilderness. The South
Bank, covered entirely in ice, is projected on the back
Olivier shutters. Light fades, leaving the National
Theatre, covered in thick ice, in a spotlight before
blackout.*

The End.

IPHIGENIA IN CRIMEA

after Euripides

Iphigenia in Crimea was first broadcast on BBC Radio 3 on 23 April 2017. The cast was as follows:

Lieutenant / Iphigenia / Athena Blake Ritson
Orestes Robert Emms
Pylades Richard Glaves
Sergeant / Thoas John Dougall
Irish Soldier / Cowherd / Chorus Eugene O'Hare
Soldier / Messenger / Chorus Michael Colgan
Soldiers / Chorus of Greek Women David Sterne,
    Gavi Singh Chera, John Bowler, Finlay Robertson

Director Emma Harding
Composer Jon Nicholls

The sounds of the Crimean War in 1854. Mortars and rifle fire.

Then a brief lull in the shelling and firing as a troop of British soldiers runs from the battle panting and swearing until they slow down and discover themselves in front of a deserted aristocratic country house in the outlying land round the besieged Sebastopol.

The group of British soldiers bursts in, finds it unoccupied.

They wonder at the interrupted rather luxurious life of the house.

SOLDIER 1

Oooo quite posh!

SOLDIER 2
Ay, posh for the Crimea.

SOLDIER 3

Hey, look there, that's champagne!

SOLDIER 4
No, mine's a beer.

SOLDIER 3

Still in its bucket and still not melted ice.
Still fizzy and not flat. (*Sips some.*) Mmm! Very nice!

SOLDIER 1

Look at that statue. Bet it's ancient bloody Greek!
I'll give them marble nipples a wee tweak.

SOLDIER 2

I think I heard that marble beauty squeak!

SOLDIER 3
Any lass 'd squeak or shriek with Jones around.
'Ere come see what randy Jones has found.

SOLDIER I
(*kissing the statue*)
'Ere come on lads, give this lass a kiss.
She likes it. She's a proper tarty miss.

There is an echoing voice repeating 'Artemis'.
The Soldiers smack kisses on the marble Artemis.
They begin to try the comfortable chairs easing
their weary bodies into comfort they are unfamiliar
with. They look around.

SOLDIER I
(*sitting in armchair*)
This is the sort of armchair t' upper classes
ease their silken pantalooned fat arses.

SOLDIER 5
I'm off upstairs to see what I can find.

Soldier 5 clatters upstairs and is heard rummaging
around.

SOLDIER I
Ah! Just the job for a gentleman's behind!

SOLDIER 3
Gentleman! Bejesus!

IRISH SOLDIER
At least I wasn't born
like you a bleeding bogside leprechaun.

SOLDIER 3
(*from upstairs*)
Hey, you lot down there. There's loads of girly gear
all posh and perfumed that I've found up here.
Come up! Come up! There's wardrobes packed.

They must have buggered off when we attacked.

All the Soldiers clatter upstairs.
Soldier 2 investigates wardrobe and reveals dresses etc. He sniffs at the crotch of a pair of pantaloons. Soldier 2 shows them to the other Soldiers.

SOLDIER 2
Here, lads, have a little sniff of that!
You can almost smell some posh girl's powdered twat.

The Soldiers all sniff and savour the fragrance.
Soldier 2 rummages more in the wardrobes.

SOLDIER 2
'Ere, Freddy, you're a titch. I bet this fits
Stuff some cloth in t'bust bits to make tits.
Put this one on. I bet it's just your size.

SOLDIER 3
(*Freddy*)
Nah! Go on, we'll all close our eyes.

Soldier 3 takes off his uniform and puts on the dress.

SOLDIER 2
Tell us when you're ready.

Pause. Rustle. Rustle.

Are you ready?

SOLDIER 3
Yes!

Soldiers open their eyes and all whistle as he reveals himself.

SOLDIER 2
Ooooo!
If I didn't know you're Freddy I'd proper fancy you.

Let's all get dresses on, and look right tarty
and give the camp a come-on concert party

> *Soldiers begin putting on dresses from wardrobe and*
> *cavorting.*
> *Exit Soldiers with all their loot.*
> *We begin to hear the sound of the song the Soldiers*
> *will sing in their dresses.*

> *British/French camp outside Sebastopol during*
> *Crimean War. A makeshift theatre, The regimental*
> *brass band is playing in the 'pit'. Soldiers dressed*
> *in looted skirts and dresses are performing*
> *flirtatiously on stage to whistles and cheers from*
> *gathered troops. They are singing a song:*

CHORUS

Sshhh! Sshhh! Sshhh! Sshhh!
What is that you hear?

> *Swish . . . swish . . . swish . . .*

Listen to our silk drawers swish
seductively in the Crimea.

> *Swish . . . swish . . . swish . . .*

I'm Moll the doll of Sebastopol,
The Fouth Division's dear!

> *Swish . . . swish . . . swish . . .*

And I'm the Balaklava belle,
(*All together.*) the cream of the Crimea!

> *Swish . . . swish . . . swish . . .*

I wink at the men in Inkerman
I blow kisses at all soldiers here!

> *Swish . . . swish . . . swish . . .*

IPHIGENIA IN CRIMEA

We send all the kisses, caresses we can,
the cream of the Crimea!

Swish . . . swish . . . swish . . .

We're the beauties behind the battlefront
and we're always revealing our rear.

Swish . . . swish . . . swish . . .

And if you're lucky you might see our . . . !
The cream of the Crimea.

*Sudden cannon fire cuts off the concert. Soldiers run
to man their own cannons, still in their skirts.*

Sergeant and Lieutenant outside Lieutenant's tent.

SERGEANT
Lieutenant, I came to check out that all's well
and nothing damaged by damned Ruski shell.

LIEUTENANT
I've been reading in my tent an ancient play
I try to read some lines from every day.
Sergeant, I'm fine and totally unhurt.
Look, there's another soldier in a skirt.
The Russians'll be amazed to see these maids
still in their dresses manning cannonades.

SERGEANT
Damned Ruski snipers up to their old game!

LIEUTENANT
Rather spoiled the concert party! Shame!

A Soldier in skirts runs past, watched by Lieutenant.

LIEUTENANT
Mademoiselles manning cannon! Not sure war 's
meant to be fought by lads in ladies' drawers.

SERGEANT

No cissies in our lot, sir! It's mostly Frogs
like trolloping about in tarty togs.

LIEUTENANT

I know their antics are a bit of mindless cheer
to lighten our spirits in the bleak Crimea.
But they could do more than simply entertain
and give us something in more serious vein.
And Euripides . . .

SERGEANT

Sorry, sir, who's he?

LIEUTENANT

Greek dramatist, fifth century BC!
He lived two millennia before
this confounded damned Crimean War
still waging here in 1854.
Euripides composed a gripping play
set in the place we find ourselves today.
He set his play *Iphigenia* here
where Brits and Ruskis fight in the Crimea.
I know you and the men don't give a toss
but the city where we're camped 's Chersonesos,
a city founded by the Greeks way back BC
when they began exploring the Black Sea.
But Sebastopol's construction meant the loss
of this two-thousand-year-old town Chersonesos.
Many a new building, library or bank
for firm foundations has Chersonesos to thank.
Wild Tartar and barbarian Muscovite
have quarried marble from this sacred site.
This broken marble column that's been made
into a makeshift but effective barricade
against the bullets that the Russian snipers spray
at us from Sebastopol day after day,
and when the peppered pillar splinters I think this,

this divine, now devastated edifice,
was the temple of the goddess Artemis
being shattered by a shower of Russian shot.
Sacred once but bang-bang now it's not!

Colonel Monroe, you know, sends his brigades
treasure-hunting with their trenching spades.
He knows beneath this bloody battleground
precious objects from the Greek past can be found,
like this I just unearthed with my boot toe,
a wine-jar handle, gold to old Monroe.

Colonel Monroe and I created our *rapport*
In Athens on our way here to the war.

SERGEANT

Ay, we saw you well-bred officers ride off
all together for your posh boys' scoff.

LIEUTENANT

We dined in the Parthenon with tables laid
for our officers in finery and braid
(none lower than lieutenant I'm afraid!)

SERGEANT

We weren't asked, sir, us poor rank and file!

LIEUTENANT

No, fine dining isn't quite your style.
And what do you lot care about Athena?

SERGEANT

We might've learned to care if we had seen her.

LIEUTENANT

Colonel Monroe and I, both classicists when young,
spoke to each other in the ancient tongue,
and in the temple of Athena, with champagne,
toasted the glory to be gained in this campaign.
We didn't want to leave but bore the loss

by remembering Greeks built Chersonesos,
the very place, this place, lest we forget,
where Euripides' *Iphigenia* 's set.
The ancient Greeks helped both of us withdraw
from the dire demands of 1854,
me into poetry, the Colonel into pots.
In old Chersonesos he's dug up lots.
Whenever the action starts abating
the Colonel sends his men out excavating.
The Colonel has what's excavated crated
to be shipped back home to be appreciated.
In every break in fighting, each small lull
his men race to get the Colonel's crates packed full,
fragments of antiquity piled high,
lamps, bronze coins, terracotta, amphorae . . .
For me when there are brief lulls in the fray
I'll read from my *Iphigenia* play.
I study the text I started at eighteen
and carried with me everywhere I've been.
In my cabin on long voyages, in my tent
the play went with me everywhere I went.
Already I know all of it by heart
and could, if called upon, play every part.
If you don't believe me, Sergeant, I'll recite
the whole damn thing in Greek one peaceful night.

SERGEANT

What an honour, sir!

LIEUTENANT
Sergeant, you're too kind!

SERGEANT
(*aside*)
You must be out of your posh little mind.

LIEUTENANT
It may seem strange but if I had my way

I'd command my regiment to do this play.
It would begin in the sun's first morning beams . . .

SERGEANT

Yes, sir! I'll put it to them!

Sergeant leaves officer in his tent.

In your fucking dreams!
Colonel Monroe obsessed wi' owt antique
and my Lieutenant gabbling bloody Greek!
Why give so much time to some crap play
set in this godforsaken shit-hole anyway.
Listen he's gone into his tent, and he'll recite
that ancient bloody Greek stuff half the night.

*Lieutenant heard reciting Euripides in Greek inside his
tent. He reaches line 18 and the word 'Agamemnon'
echoes in the air.*

LIEUTENANT
(thinking)

That would be a marvellous idea
to put Iphigenia on right here
where she was priestess of the holy shrine
of Artemis, now rubble. The main role's mine!
Seeing the squaddies all dressed up as tarts
reminds me men played all the female parts
as well as all the male parts way back then
in Athens for an audience of men.
And men is all we've got, and so it seems
to finally fulfil my deepest dreams
I put on appropriate female attire
and make my deep male voice a wee bit higher
and enter before you all, Iphigenia.

*Lieutenant puts on dress and practises voice, then
enters as Iphigenia.*

IPHIGENIA

Pelops, son of Tantalus, set off for Pisa
with his speedy steeds and wed Hippodamia;
Atreus was her son, and Atreus's sons were
Menelaus, and the Agamemnon I sprang from,
child of Clytemnestra, Iphigenia . . .

Lieutenant/Iphigenia stops.

LIEUTENANT

The vocal part's not easy for us men.
Give me a moment and I'll start again.

Lieutenant works on his voice.

LIEUTENANT

It would help me if I hear when I come in
a loud drumroll for the drama's heroine.

Drumroll.
   Lieutenant enters again as Iphigenia.

IPHIGENIA

Pelops, son of Tantalus, set off for Pisa
with his speedy steeds and wed Hippodamia;
Atreus was her son, and Atreus's sons were
Menelaus, and the Agamemnon I sprang from,
child of Clytemnestra, Iphigenia,
by wind-churned dark eddies of Euripus
sacrificed . . . slaughtered . . . my throat slit
for Helen's sake, by my father (so-called!
my throat . . . my father . . . sacrificing to Artemis
by the now notorious inlets of Aulis.
There Agamemnon, the king, had assembled his fleet
of a thousand ships, hoping to win for the Greeks
a victor's wreath for Troy, and take revenge
on Helen's violated vows, to pacify Menelaus.
When the right breeze wasn't blowing for the fleet to sail
the king burnt sacrifices, and priest Calchas spoke:

'Lord of the Greek host, Agamemnon, you'll launch
   no ships
and the voyage won't happen till your vows are fulfilled,
and Artemis is given your daughter Iphigenia,
sacrificed to the goddess as you swore in your vow.
You swore to the light-bearing goddess you'd offer
the fairest fruit that the year would bring forth
and your wife Clytemnestra has a child at home.'
(I got 'fairest fruit' prize from Calchas the priest!)
'And she must be offered as a sacrifice now.'
So the sly tricks of Odysseus got me from my mother.
His pretence was I'd be the bride of Achilles.
Once they'd got me to Aulis, up, up I was lifted
over the altar to be given the knife thrust.
But the goddess Artemis snatched me away
by switching my body for that of a deer
and the Greeks slit the deer's throat instead of my own.
She flew me through the bright sky here
to the land of the Taurians, barbarians,
even their king who runs like he had wings,
which is why he's called Thoas, fleet of foot.
Artemis made me priestess of her temple
to officiate over her festival rites,
barbarian rites from before my arrival,
and 'festival's a fair word with fear underneath.
By these 'festive' rites I've got to sacrifice
any Greek who lands here on these shores.
I sacrifice (as I was, almost, at Aulis)
any Greek who lands here in Crimea.

Pause.

If I tell the sky the bad dreams of last night
it might in the telling bring some relief.
I dreamed I'd changed lands and was back home in Argos.
I was asleep in the palace where girls had their quarters.
An earthquake shook the ground underneath me.

Then I was outside and saw, or dreamed I saw,
a roof cornice tumble, and then the whole roof,
the columns all crashing down to the ground.
There was only one left standing, and it seemed
to have a head on it with darkish auburn hair.
It seemed to speak, and I, who kill strangers here,
sprinkled water on it, doomed to die, and wept.
This is what I think that bad dream means:
Orestes is dead. It was him I sprinkled water on.
Sons are a house's pillars. Those I sprinkle die.
My long absent brother needs a libation
and I'll pour one, though we're oceans apart.
That's the least I can do. My servants will help me.
Those Greek women King Thoas gave me,
for some reason or other don't seem to be here.
I'll go inside here where my duties are done,
my place as the priestess of Artemis.
The goddess who saved me I now have to serve.

Exit Iphigenia. Enter Orestes and Pylades.

ORESTES

Watch out in case someone comes and we're spied.

PYLADES

Orestes, my eyes are peeled. I'll check each side.

ORESTES

The goddess's temple? Pylades, could this be
what we came from Argos for across the sea?

PYLADES

You should believe it. It looks like it to me.

ORESTES

And there the altar where Greek gore drips down?

PYLADES

The cornices are stained with dried blood brown.

ORESTES

And look there, dangling trophies, swarming with flies.

PYLADES

The skulls of killed Greeks with no flesh or eyes.
I'll check if there's somewhere we can get in by.

Pylades checks out the temple.

ORESTES

This net you've got me trapped in, Apollo, why?
I'm here on your orders after killing my mother.
She killed my father. I killed her. Then these Furies'
constant tormentings drove me from my homeland.
I'd gone round in circles then went to Delphi
to ask how I could finish this suffering, these frenzies.
You said I should come to the Crimea's borders
where your sister Artemis possesses her altars
and take that image of her that fell here from the sky,
by some sly way or other. Then, that ordeal over,
I had to give it to the land of the Athenians.
(What they'd do with the image you chose not to say.)
This done, my suffering, finally, would find some relief.
So I've obeyed all your orders and find myself here
somewhere in Crimea, clearly quite hostile.

To Pylades.

So, Pylades, what do you think we should do?
Do we need ladders to get us up there?
If we climb up that high we're bound to be seen.
Or can we bludgeon the door-bolts open with bars?
If they catch us, though, battering the temple doors
and forcing an entrance, we're bound to be killed.
So let's quit and creep back to the ship we came in on.

PYLADES

Flight's not on, Orestes! Flight's not the Greek way.
We mustn't make light of Apollo's commandment.

Let's leave the temple and hide in the caves
the black sea's waves wash in and out of.
We'll keep away from the ship in case someone spots it
and reports to these princes and gets us captured.
But once the night has shown its gloomy face
we'll steel ourselves and find some trick or other
to get the image of Artemis out of this temple.
The brave get things done. No one likes cowards.

ORESTES

You're right, of course, Pylades. I've got to agree!
We'll find some place close by to lie low in.
I'd be the last to want Apollo frustrated.
Yes, we'll steel ourselves. We're young. No excuses!

*Temple door opens. Chorus of Women begins to
emerge.*

Look, women, coming out of the temple. Let's hide!

*Exit Orestes and Pylades.
    Enter Chorus. Laughter from troops, whistles etc.
which die down once they realise the Chorus has
serious things to say.*

CHORUS

Sshhh! Sshhh! Sshhh! Sshhh!
All of you assembled here
this side of the Symplegades,
the clashing cleft, in the Crimea.

Artemis, Artemis in your temple there,
we serve Iphigenia who keeps the key,
the priestess you carried through the air
not like us shipped over the sea.

Forced to quit sacked city towers,
forced out of house and home,
out of the Greece that once was ours,
trafficked across the Black Sea foam.

With husbands, fathers, sons all left
unburied where they died,
captives trafficked through the clashing cleft
to the Black Sea's barbaric side.

Once we'd seen the slave ship scrape
through the clashing cleft, Symplegades,
we're in the Crimea with no escape,
no rescuing Greeks who'd cross these seas.

Green meadows, woods, the Greece we miss,
as captives in Crimea,
serving the priestess of Artemis
a goddess made crueller here.

Enter Iphigenia.

Serving this priestess of Artemis,
a gore-goddess in Crimea.
We've come. Has something happened?
What's on your mind?
Why have you brought me to the temple,
daughter of Agamemnon who went to Troy's towers
with a thousand ships and ten thousand armed soldiers?

IPHIGENIA

My attendants!
My voice can't make more than harsh lamentations
strangled by stringless sounds
no Greek lyre ever made.
In grieving cries – Agh! . . . Agh! . . .
Screams coming in between keening . . .
grieving and keening for Orestes, my brother.
His apparition appeared in my nightmare
that came in the darkness that's just passed away.

I'm done for! I'm done for!
Agh! . . . Agh! . . . All my kin vanished!
Agh! . . . Agh! . . . All that suffering in Argos!

You divine power
who sent my brother to Hades.
It's for him I'll wet the ground with libations
poured from a bowl meant for the departed,
first milk from hill-grazing cows,
wine-draughts from Bacchus
and that made by the labour of bees –
milk, wine, honey give dead spirits comfort.
Hand me the gold bowl
I'll pour liquid from down to Hades.

Son of Agamemnon under the ground,
these libations are for you. My dead brother!
Take them! I won't be able to bring you
a tress, or my tear-drops – you don't have a tomb.
I've been brought far away from our homeland
where they believe I'm dead with my throat slit.

CHORUS

The frenzy of grief keeps our cries crude and raw
the music of Hades with no joy in its cadence.
Music to mourn the dead in the shrillest of dirges.
Agh! . . . Agh . . . Agh . . . the house of the Atreids,
the light gone, the sceptre gone . . . Agh . . . Agh!

Murder on murder, anguish on anguish
for the family of Tantalus from long ago.
That family's bloodshed brings taint to yours.
Some power, some Fury hatches ruin for you.

IPHIGENIA

My star's been an ill one right from the start,
from my mother's womb even, the very start.
The fates who presided over my birthing
forced me into a life full of anguish,
me, first born to Clytemnestra, daughter of Leda,
brought up to further a father's blood-letting.
In a horse-drawn carriage they brought me

a doomed bride to the sea-shore at Aulis
intended as the wife of Achilles. (Agh!)
Now a stranger I live in a house that's forbidding
here on the sea that's been dubbed 'the unfriendly'–
manless, childless, cityless. Friendless,
me who had suitors from all over Hellas.
I never sang the sweet songs for Hera in Argos
nor on the chattering loom do I depict
with my shuttle the likeness of Pallas and Titans.
No, instead, I inflict a bloody fate
our Greek lyre has no voice for, on strangers
who cry out in terror and shed piteous tears.
Now I've emptied my head of them all
I weep for my brother now dead in Argos,
you, the one I left still little and gentle
in your mother's arms suckling at her breast,
the future ruler of Argos, a baby. Orestes.

CHORUS

Look, there's a cowherd running up from the shore.
It looks like there's something he wants you to know.

COWHERD

Daughter of Agamemnon and Clytemnestra,
listen to the strange tale I've got to relate.

IPHIGENIA

What can be so pressing for you to interrupt?

COWHERD

Newcomers! Newcomers here in our land.
Their ship managed to dodge the dark Symplegades.
Two young men together, just the right thing
to offer as sacrifice to Crimean Artemis.
Be ready to sprinkle the goddess's victims.

IPHIGENIA

Where are they from? Did their looks give some clue?

COWHERD

They're Greeks, I'd say, by the looks of them two?

IPHIGENIA

Did you hear names being used for either of these?

COWHERD

One called the other one Pylades.

IPHIGENIA

What name did the one who was with him go by?

COWHERD

The others heard no name. Neither did I.

IPHIGENIA

Whereabouts did you grab them these strangers you saw?

COWHERD

Where the unfriendly sea-waves break on the shore.

IPHIGENIA

Why were you on the beach though, you're cattlemen?

COWHERD

Our cows get a washdown down there now and then.

IPHIGENIA

Go back to the capture! Where, how and when?
How did you manage this? Please let me know.
It's a long time since the goddess's altar
has been reddened with the blood-daubs of Greeks.

COWHERD

We were driving our cattle that graze on these woodlands
towards the sea that flows through the Symplegades.
There's a cave there constant waves have made hollow
where men hunt for shellfish they crush to make purple.
One of us cowherds caught a glimpse of two youths.
He tiptoed back to tell us what he'd stumbled across.
'Can't you see 'em, over there? Gods by the look!'

Then one of us, a god-fearing bloke, looked at them both
and started a prayer: 'Son of sea goddess Leucothea,
protector of ships Palaemon be propitious!
whether it's Castor and Pollux who sit on our shores
or the loved sons of Nereus who begot the fifty-strong
chorus of Nereids who ride waves and guide ships . . .'

But another, a bit outspoken in his lack of belief,
laughed at the prayer and said: 'They're shipwrecked
    sailors!
They're crouched in the rock-cleft as they've heard of
    our custom
of sacrificing strangers and clearly they're scared.'
Most of us thought he spoke sense so decided
to catch them and sacrifice them as is our custom.
While we made plans one of the strangers left the rocks
and stood, his head shaking up and down, moaning,
his fingers twitching, convulsed by mad fits.
Then he shouted out with a voice like a hunter:
'Pylades, look at that one, that she-snake from Hades.
Don't you see her? There! There! She's trying to kill me,
flailing at me with a whiplash of vipers.
This one oozes blood, oozes fire, wings whirring and
    flapping,
holding in her arms my mother's carved image,
a huge weight of marble to crack my skull open.
No! No! She'll kill me. Where will I run to?'
We could see nothing. No sea-snakes. No monsters.
All we could hear was cows mooing, dogs barking.
Reckoning he was croaking, we just crouch there in
    silence.
But he draws his sword and leaps on our cattle
like a lion, slashes their flanks, jabs steel in their ribs,
making the sea-spume blossom with blood,
thinking he was hacking not cattle but Furies,
while we all stand there watching our herd being
    slaughtered.

We get ourselves weapons and blow on our conch-shells
to alert others to help because we realised we didn't
against those trained youthful strangers stand much of
   a chance.
Soon we'd gathered a reasonable number.
The foreigner collapses as his madness receded,
his chops were all slobbery, and when we see him fallen
to a man we start chucking rocks at the strangers.
But the other foreigner wipes his friend's face of slaver
and shields his body with his thick woven cloak
making sure our missiles went wide of their mark,
protecting his friend with an unselfish kindness.
When he came to his senses he leaped to his feet
and saw the numbers attacking and groaned aloud
and went on being pelted with pebbles and stones.

Then we heard this scary sort of rallying cry.
'We're going to die, Pylades. But let's die like heroes.
In the noblest way we can. Draw your sword. Follow me.'
We saw their blades being brandished and we fled.
We ran away and huddled down in a gully.
But if some of us fled there were others kept pelting,
and if they get driven back the ones who retreated
rally and hurl their rocks at the strangers.
But (this is the strange bit!) though they hurled many
   missiles
no one managed to hit the goddess's victims.
With some effort, and not before time, we prevailed.
We surrounded them and knocked their swords from
   their grasp
with a barrage of stones. They sank to their knees
exhausted. And we brought them at once to the king.
As soon as he saw them he said take them to you
to be ritually anointed and then sacrificed.
I'd be glad of strangers like these for my sacrifices
so Greece gets paid back for your murder at Aulis.

CHORUS
Quite a story you've told – these Greeks turning up,
whoever they are, braving the hostile Black Sea.

IPHIGENIA
Well, go and fetch the strangers here
and I'll see to it that things are made ready.

My desperate heart, once compassionate and gentle
towards strangers, with tears for those closest in kin
when it was Greeks who fell into your hands.
The bad dreams of last night have made me hard-hearted
and you'll find me pitiless whoever you are.

(*To Chorus.*)
Dear friends, this is a truth I've discovered:
when those who have suffered meet the more fortunate
because of their suffering they don't wish them well.
No wind sent by Zeus has blown here ever yet
a vessel bearing Helen through the Symplegades,
Helen, the cause of my destruction, and Menelaus,
so I could make them pay for their crimes,
an Aulis for an Aulis, one here and one there,
where I was hoisted like a calf to get my throat slit
by the Greeks, by that throat-slitter my father.
I'll never forget the horrors of that terrible moment.
Time after time my hand touched his cheek
and kept saying 'Father, through you I'm a bride
in a base betrothal. And as you slit my throat
my mother and the women of Argos are singing
my wedding hymn, the palace loud with flute-players
and serenaded by bride-song I'm butchered by you.
Achilles was no son of Peleus. His father was Hades.
And this son of Hades you offered as husband,
carried me in a conveyance to the bloody bridal,
a wedding veil over my face covering my eyes.
I never lifted my brother (the one who's dead) into my
    arms,

I never kissed my young sister out of shame and
   abashment
that I was bound for the palace of Peleus.
I put off those warm hugs till I came back to Argos.
O poor Orestes, if you are dead, all those fine 'qualities'
passed on by our father you're going to miss out on.
And I find it slightly more than confusing
that Artemis is a goddess noted for wisdom.
If one of us mortals makes contact with bloodshed
or touches a corpse or handles a childbirth
she bans them from her altars as being polluted
and yet she seems to take pleasure in men sacrificed.
How could Leto, Zeus's consort,
ever give birth to such barbaric ideas?
I don't believe Tantalus fed the gods child-flesh.
Would any deity banquet on boy-meat?
The barbarians here though, being bloodthirsty, transfer
their flaw to the goddess I'm supposed to be serving.
It's my belief no god could ever be evil.

CHORUS

The gadfly with buzzing Black Sea whine
goaded Io across dark seas,
through Europe/Asia's dividing line,
the clashing cleft, Symplegades.

What goaded these Greeks with hands tied
to leave sweet Greece to suffer this,
Crimea, the Black Sea's savage side
with blood-demanding Artemis?

Was greed for gold these Greeks' gadfly?
A greed starts small but soon can grow
impossible to gratify
wherever or how far they go.

Or how many ports sail to and sack
or how much bullion they load.

The Symplegades won't keep them back
with greed for gold their gadfly goad.

Iphigenia begs fate to summon
Helen from Troy to the Crimea
so she can kill the guilty woman
in the manner practised here.

Helen, who caused the whole Trojan War,
her gold ringlets would be sprayed
with gushes of hot gizzard gore
from Iphigenia's blade.

But far more I wish that fate would send
rescuing Greeks to the Crimea
to bring our enslavement to an end,
an end to this slave-life and fear,

back in my city, my home, and free
to dance and sing in a group like this,
Greek jubilation not Black Sea
barbarity for Artemis.

The strangers the cowherd told us he'd found,
sacrifices for Artemis inside there,
look they're here that Greek pair bound.
Keep silence first, then utter our prayer.

Silence.

Gifts, Artemis, you don't abhor
in this barbaric Black Sea land,
your altar stained with strangers' gore,
back home in Greece we'd brand
unholy, and beyond the law
back in the Greece we knew before.
Back home in Greece . . . Back home in Greece . . .

IPHIGENIA

First I'll make sure all's in order for the goddess.
But release the strangers' hands

As they are sacred they musn't be bound.
Go inside the temple and get things prepared.
Get everything needed for what must be done.

Exit Chorus.

Aagggh!

To Orestes and Pylades.

Who was your mother, your father? Does a sister exist?
Such a double loss for her – both her brothers.
Who can know when baleful things will befall?
The gods' plans are obscure . . .
Where do you hail from, wretched strangers?
To reach here you must have spent a long time at sea
but not as long as you'll spend under ground.

ORESTES
Woman (I don't know your name) whoever you are,
why disturb yourself over our problems not yours?
Odd that someone about to commit execution
should show some compassion to diminish the terror.
And a condemned man's stupid to grieve when all's
    hopeless.
Stupid twice over. He shows his stupidity and dies anyway.
We should let fortune take her course.
Don't mourn us. We know what goes on here,
the sacrifices that are made. We understand.

IPHIGENIA
Which one is Pylades out of you two?

ORESTES
He is. But why should that matter to you?

IPHIGENIA
Where in Greece was he born, this Pylades?

ORESTES
I don't see the point of questions like these?

IPHIGENIA

So maybe you're brothers of the same blood?

ORESTES

No, it's friendship binds us in our brotherhood.

IPHIGENIA

And what kind of name did *your* father bestow?

ORESTES

It should have been 'Luckless'. That name suits my woe.

IPHIGENIA

Not my question. It's to fate your complaint should
    be made.

ORESTES

It's my body not my name you'll slash with your blade.

IPHIGENIA

Why grudge me it? Too proud, that's clear.

ORESTES

A nameless dead man is one you can't smear.

IPHIGENIA

And your city? I suppose that's secret too.

ORESTES

I'm doomed to die. What do I gain if I share it with you?

IPHIGENIA

But what stops you doing it out of good grace?

ORESTES

I'm proud to claim Argos as my birthplace.

IPHIGENIA

Really, stranger? Argos? Is that really true?

ORESTES

Yes, from Mycenae, a city once all Hellas knew.

IPHIGENIA

If you're from Argos it's good you've come here.

ORESTES

Good for you, maybe, but not me, I fear.

IPHIGENIA

Was it something else or was it exile you got?

ORESTES

You could call it exile, half-wanted, half not.

IPHIGENIA

There's something I'd like you, please, to explain.

ORESTES

O why not? It'll help me forget about pain.

IPHIGENIA

Of Troy and its stories you're no doubt aware?

ORESTES

I wish that I wasn't. It's still my nightmare.

IPHIGENIA

They say that Troy's finished, ruined by war.

ORESTES

It's true what they say. Yes. Troy is no more.

IPHIGENIA

Did Menelaus and Helen, his wife, reunite?

ORESTES

Yes, but for my kinsman her return proved a blight.

IPHIGENIA

Where's Helen now who hasn't yet paid me back for
her sin?

ORESTES

Sparta! Her former spouse took her back in.

IPHIGENIA
All Greeks detest her. I'm not alone.

ORESTES
Her marriage gave me great gifts of my own!

IPHIGENIA
And the Greeks got back as the stories all say?

ORESTES
You'll get the whole epic if you grill me this way.

IPHIGENIA
I need all the details before you must die.

ORESTES
Then ask me and I'll answer or at least try.

IPHIGENIA
Did Calchas the prophet get back from the war?

ORESTES
The news in Mycenae is that he's no more.

IPHIGENIA
O Artemis, that's good news. Odysseus? Is he?

ORESTES
Alive! Not back home. Still somewhere at sea.

IPHIGENIA
May he stay there and die there, that is my curse.

ORESTES
They say the life of Odysseus couldn't get worse.

IPHIGENIA
And Achilles, son of Thetis? Did he survive Troy?

ORESTES
No! His wedding at Aulis brought him no joy.

IPHIGENIA
A sham as those who suffered at Aulis soon knew.

ORESTES

This need to know about Greece? Who are you? Who?

IPHIGENIA

I'm from there! But was ruined and left long ago.

ORESTES

Now it makes sense why you're desperate to know.

IPHIGENIA

So what of the general they called 'lucky-starred'?

ORESTES

To fit that name on who I know would be very hard.

IPHIGENIA

Agamemnon the king is the one meant by this.

ORESTES

I know nothing. Let's give that subject a miss.

IPHIGENIA

No, by the gods, I beg you. I need to know.

ORESTES

He's dead. And his death caused others great woe.

IPHIGENIA

Dead? Dead? What disaster? Say it's not true!

ORESTES

Why wail? What was Agamemnon to you?

IPHIGENIA

I'm lamenting a fall from a 'lucky-starred' life?

ORESTES

His death was terrible. Hacked down by his wife.

IPHIGENIA

Pitiable! Pitiable! Both for hacker and hacked.

ORESTES

Stop there! Don't try to nag me for one more fact.

IPHIGENIA

Just this one. That ill-starred man's wife. Is she still there?

ORESTES

No! Butchered by the son she'd been happy to bear.

IPHIGENIA

Her son? House of torments! Her son killed her? Why?

ORESTES

She'd killed his father. So she had to die.

IPHIGENIA

What a wrong but just fate for him to fulfil.

ORESTES

For all it's justice the gods still treat him ill.

IPHIGENIA

Agamemnon's children? Were there more than this son?

ORESTES

A daughter called Electra's now the last one.

IPHIGENIA

The one who was sacrificed? What of that daughter?

ORESTES

Nothing, except that they took her for slaughter.

IPHIGENIA

Poor child! And poor father who wielded the knife.

ORESTES

It was through evil Helen that child lost her life.

IPHIGENIA

The dead king's son? Is Argos his home?

ORESTES

No, everywhere. Nowhere, in frenzy, forced to roam.

IPHIGENIA

So much for my nightmares I now know are false.

ORESTES

So too the gods though reputed for wisdom
are no more to be trusted either than dreams.

IPHIGENIA

Listen! I've just thought of a plan.
A plan to your advantage, strangers, and to mine.
It's best when the same thing satisfies both.
Would you be willing, if I rescue you,
to go to Argos with a message for those I love there,
to carry a letter I asked a captive to write?
This captive didn't hold me guilty of his death.
He thought it was custom that was taking his life,
and accepted the rite of Artemis as just.
I've had no one I could send, once spared, to Argos
to take my letter to one of my loved ones back there.
But you seem not low-born and know Mycenae
and it's with there I need contact. So be spared.
Claim what's not a measly reward – being spared
for conveying this writing that weighs almost nothing.
And since the people here force this to happen
let your friend be the goddess's victim not you.

ORESTES

Your plan seems a good one but for one thing.
For this man to be killed would weigh on my heart.
He only sails with me because of my troubles.
I couldn't just destroy him to gain your good grace,
and escape myself from pain. Let it be like this:
give him the letter, and he'll deliver it to Argos.
Then you'll have all that you've wanted.
Then let the one who wants the sacrifice kill me.
It's shameful to dump your friends to save yourself.
The life of my friend here's as precious as my own.

IPHIGENIA

I admire your courage. Your stock must be noble.
You show your friend friendship at its most true.
If my brother's alive I hope he's like you.
Yes, I too have a brother, though not one I see.
If that's what you want. He takes the letter. You die.
There's some deep drive within you for wanting it so.

ORESTES

My sacrifice? The dark deed? Who'll be the one?

IPHIGENIA

Me! The goddess demands I get the deed done.

ORESTES

That won't bring much luck or envy your way.

IPHIGENIA

I have no choice. There are orders I have to obey.

ORESTES

A male killed by a female, me killed by you?

IPHIGENIA

No! Anointing you with water. That's what I do.

ORESTES

If you don't do the killing tell me who will.

IPHIGENIA

They're inside the temple, those chosen to kill.

ORESTES

What rites will my corpse get once life has left?

IPHIGENIA

Sacred fire inside then a deep rocky cleft.

ORESTES

Arghh! My corpse not made ready by my sister's hand.

IPHIGENIA

She lives a long way from this barbarous land,

so to want that's vain, poor man, whoever you are.
But because you happen to be Argos born
I myself will give you what brief rites I can.
I'll bestow some adornment when you are buried
and moisten your body with bright yellow oil,
and drizzle honey from mountain bees on to your pyre.
I must bring the letter from out of the temple.
So that you don't feel any more hostile to me –
Guard them, but loosen the rope round their hands.
It will be a surprise the news that I'm sending
to my loved ones in Argos, one loved above all.
This letter saying those he thought dead are alive
will bring him a joy he couldn't have looked for.

Iphigenia goes into the temple.

ORESTES
Pylades, do you have the same feelings as me?

PYLADES
Tell me what they are and then we can see.

ORESTES
This young woman, who is she? How Greek she seemed.
Those questions! The suffering at Troy. The return to
   Greece.
Or Calchas who knew bird-lore, and Achilles of fame.
How upset she seemed about poor Agamemnon.
And she asked me about his wife and his children.
She's an Argive, this stranger. Her birthplace is Argos.
Or she wouldn't send this letter or ask us such questions,
as though her welfare depended on the welfare of Argos.

PYLADES
You've taken the words right out of my mouth.
I'd say one thing though. It's pretty common knowledge
the sufferings of Greek kings, the destruction of Troy.
But there's another thing I need to say . . .

ORESTES

Say it! And we can discuss it together.

PYLADES

It would shame me to go on living if you die.
We shared the voyage here. We should share our death.
I'll be accused of cowardice, my behaviour branded
both in Argos and all the valleys of Phocis.
They'll all believe (you know what they're like)
that I got back only by a best friend's betrayal,
contriving your fate for the sake of the kingship,
married as I am to your sister, the heiress.
This makes me afraid and feel full of shame.
It's only right that I breathe my last at your side,
be slaughtered with you, my corpse burned with yours.
I'm your friend. I'd loathe to be branded your betrayer.

ORESTES

Don't talk like that! My burdens are mine to bear.
But I have enough trouble without adding yours.
What you call shameful, what you call full of pain,
is the same as I'd feel if I caused your death,
when you've been so loyal and brave at my side.
Faring as the gods have made me fare so far
it's no bad thing for me to leave this life behind.
But you, you're thriving, your house isn't polluted
or diseased, unlike mine, impious, cursed with bad luck.
If you are spared you'll have sons by my sister
who I gave you as spouse, and my ancestral line
won't be wiped out through lack of descendants.
Go! Live! Settle in the house of my father
and when you come to Greece and the Argos of horses
I enjoin you by this right hand to do as follows:
raise a mound. Make it stand as my memorial
and let my sister weep and place hair on this grave.
Tell her I was killed by a woman from Argos,
purified and sacrificed on the altar of Artemis.

Never desert Electra for all the taint of the household.
Farewell! Of all my friends I loved you the most.
We hunted together. We grew up together.
And you've borne with me so much of my burden.
Apollo the prophet has cheated me by a trick,
driven me as far out of Greece as he could
ashamed of the prophecies which never came true.
I trusted him with everything. I listened. I obeyed.
I killed my mother, now I'm the one murdered!

PYLADES

You'll have your grave. I won't betray your Electra.
My poor friend, I'll love you more dead than alive.
Apollo's prophecy hasn't destroyed you yet
even though balanced on the cliff-edge of death.
It happens, it does happen that huge misfortune
can give way suddenly and then be reversed.

ORESTES

No more! Apollo's word 's no use to me.
Here comes the woman out of the temple.

Enter Iphigenia.

IPHIGENIA

Go help them prepare the sacrifice inside.

Exit Chorus.

Here's the letter with its many leaves, strangers.
But listen to what I need from you further.
When a man's out of trouble his boldness comes back.
Now you are frightened, I fear once you're free
and out of this country and safely back home
you won't give another thought to my letter.

ORESTES

What do you want? What is it you're needing?

IPHIGENIA

Let him swear me an oath that he'll take the letter
I give him to Argos and to those it's meant for.

ORESTES

And will you on your part swear an oath too?

IPHIGENIA

What must I swear that I'll do or not do?

ORESTES

He'll be released from this barbarous country alive.

IPHIGENIA

How else could my letter hope to arrive?

ORESTES

And the king of this country will he agree?

IPHIGENIA

Yes!
  And your friend will board ship escorted by me.

ORESTES

So what is the oath my friend here must swear?

IPHIGENIA

'To your loved ones in Greece this letter I'll bear.'

PYLADES

'To your loved ones in Greece this letter I'll bear.'

IPHIGENIA

You'll pass the Dark Rocks and safely reach there.

PYLADES

Which of the gods did you swear your oath by?

IPHIGENIA

Artemis, in whose temple my duties still lie.

PYLADES

And I by great Zeus who rules earth and sky.

IPHIGENIA

And if that bond's broken and you prove untrue . . .?

PYLADES

I'll never see home. And if my life's not saved by you?

IPHIGENIA

That Argos I long for may I never see.

PYLADES

We've overlooked something it seems to me.

IPHIGENIA

If it's a good thing let us all know . . .

PYLADES

Promise me one thing. If something happens to the ship
and the letter goes to the bottom along with your message,
and only I survive from the shipwreck
the oath I've sworn you won't still be binding.

IPHIGENIA

I'll tell you everything the letter has in it
so you can repeat it to my loved ones in Argos.
That makes things safe. If it gets there still intact
it will give its message out silently.
But if the letter ends up in the sea,
if you save yourself you'll save my words.

PYLADES

Good idea! We both gain. But tell me this:
It's for someone in Argos, this letter, who?
Or who say the words to once learned from you?

IPHIGENIA

Say to Orestes son of Agamemnon
that she whose throat was slit at Aulis sends these words,
Iphigenia, who's alive though to them is departed.

ORESTES

Where is she, then? Has she come back from the dead?

IPHIGENIA

She's here! You're looking at her. But don't interrupt.
'Bring me to Argos, brother, from this barbarous land
where I have to kill strangers, before I die.'

ORESTES

What's going on? Where on earth is this place?

IPHIGENIA
(*continuing*)

'Or I'll raise a curse against your whole house,
Orestes.' I'll say it again so you remember.

ORESTES

Gods!

IPHIGENIA

Why call on the gods when I'm speaking?

ORESTES

No reason! Continue. I was somewhere else.
Soon I won't need more questions to know everything.

IPHIGENIA

Say that the goddess Artemis saved my life
by putting a deer in my place for my father to slaughter
and made it look like it was my throat he was slitting.
She settled me here. That's what's in the letter.

PYLADES

They're easy to keep the oaths that I swore
and take no time at all to bring to fulfilment.
Orestes, take this letter sent by your sister.

ORESTES

So I will, but I'll lay the letter aside.
The joy that I feel needs no more words.
Dearest sister, I'm struck dumb. Dumb.

But I embrace you in my stunned disbelief.
The news that I've heard makes me ecstatic.

IPHIGENIA
Stranger, your touch taints the goddess's servant,
throwing your arms round her sacrosanct garments.

ORESTES
My own dear sister, child of one father,
Agamemnon! It's me, don't turn away.
You hold the brother you never thought you would hold.

IPHIGENIA
You! My brother! Stop such wild talk.
My brother is in Argos if he's anywhere.

ORESTES
Poor woman, that's not where your brother is now.

IPHIGENIA
It was the Spartan daughter of Tyndareus bore you.

ORESTES
To the grandson of Pelops who was my father.

IPHIGENIA
What are you saying? Do you have any proof?

ORESTES
Yes! But test me on questions about our old home?

IPHIGENIA
Why don't I just listen to you telling me?

ORESTES
Electra must have told you of the tensions
that existed between Thyestes and Atreus.

IPHIGENIA
I heard they quarrelled over some golden lamb.

ORESTES
Yes, and you know you wove it into a hanging.

IPHIGENIA

Dear one, your words come close to striking a chord.

ORESTES

And you wove sunrise into the hanging as well.

IPHIGENIA

I wove it into a textile of fine threads.

ORESTES

And the water our mother sent to bathe you at Aulis?

IPHIGENIA

The bliss of my bridal didn't make me forget it!

ORESTES

And the locks of your hair that were sent to our mother?

IPHIGENIA

They were to be buried instead of my body,

ORESTES

Now I'll give you more proofs, things I remember:
The spear in my father's house belonging to Pelops
he killed Oenomaus with to win Hippodamia of Pisa.
The spear was kept in the rooms where you girls slept.

IPHIGENIA

Dearest, dearest no more, no more. I hold you
I hold you, Orestes, too long far from home,
far from Argos, the homeland, my dear one.

ORESTES

And I hold you who I long thought was dead.

IPHIGENIA

A tear, a sob wets my cheek in joy . . .

ORESTES

Mine too!

IPHIGENIA

When I left you were a babe in your mother's arms,

(The pride of the palace)
O luck much luckier than words can express!
What can I say?
Beyond all marvels, beyond all words
has all this turned out.

ORESTES
In future may we be lucky together.

IPHIGENIA
O friends, I've found extraordinary joy.
I'm afraid it will fly off into the air.
Hail Cyclopean hearth, dear Mycenae, dear homeland.
I thank you for his life, and his nurture,
this brother of mine, the light of the house.

ORESTES
In our birth we were blessed but not in our lives,
sister, and in all we have suffered.

IPHIGENIA
The suffering! The suffering! How my dark-souled
father thrust his knife at my throat.

ORESTES
I can see it, I can see it, though I wasn't at Aulis.

IPHIGENIA
There were no hymns when they brought me
to the sham, bogus bride-bed of Achilles.
At the altar there were tears, there were groans,
Aaaggh! Those anointings! Those anointings! Aaaagh!

ORESTES
I cry too at what our father committed.

IPHIGENIA
Fatherly kindness wasn't my life lot
but now something different, some fortune god-sent.

ORESTES

Supposing, poor wretch, you'd butchered your brother?

IPHIGENIA

Terrible things I did, I did terrible things.
Ah, my brother, you escaped by a whisker.
You escaped an unholy death at my hands.
How will it all end? What future can I expect?
What way can I find for you out of the city
away from your death and back to Argos our homeland
before the sacrificial blade lets out your blood?
The problem, poor soul, is for you to solve.
Overland! Not by ship but by fleetness of foot.
You'll pass close to death through barbarian tribes
and endless tracks that seem to lead nowhere.
But through the narrow gaps in the Dark Rocks
is a long voyage by ship.
What god, what mortal, what unlooked for event
will give us a route through this dead end?
And show a way for these two descendents of Atreus
to be released from their torment?

PYLADES

When long-lost loved ones come face to face,
Orestes, it's only natural they want to embrace,
but let's leave off lamenting and face up to things.
How shall we win now the prize of salvation?
How get ourselves out of this barbarous land?
This is the wise way, hang on to good fortune
but seize the moment and increase that good fortune.

ORESTES

You've spoken well. I think we depend on fortune
as well as ourselves. I think divine power
aids those the most who show the most spirit . . .

IPHIGENIA

One question though you won't stop me from asking.
Our sister Electra? How does she fare?

ORESTES

Well. Very well. She's married to Pylades there.

IPHIGENIA

Where 's he from? Whose son? If I may enquire.

ORESTES

His birthplace is Phocis, and Strophius his sire.

IPHIGENIA

His mother's our aunt, so we're bloodkin, us two.

ORESTES

He's your cousin. And my one friend who's stayed true.

IPHIGENIA

He wasn't born when our father killed me.

ORESTES

No, Strophius was late starting his own family.

IPHIGENIA

My dear sister's husband, salutations to you.

ORESTES

Salute not just my kinsman, my guardian too.

Pause.

IPHIGENIA

Our mother? That dire deed? How did you dare?

ORESTES

Revenge for our father. Let's leave it there.

IPHIGENIA

Our mother killed our father? Why? Why? Why?

ORESTES

I said leave it there. Best not to pry.

IPHIGENIA

I'll say no more? But Argos, you're now in command?

ORESTES

No, Menelaus. We're both in exile from our native land.

IPHIGENIA

Would our uncle foul further our fouled family?

ORESTES

No, fear of the Furies. That made me flee.

IPHIGENIA

Ah, harried by Furies! Mother-murder 's the cause.

ORESTES

They forced their bloody horse-bit into my jaws.

IPHIGENIA

It was them then, that fit the cattlemen saw?

ORESTES

Many have witnessed that same fit before.

IPHIGENIA

Why choose this country as part of your quest?

ORESTES

I came to this country at Apollo's behest.

IPHIGENIA

And what did Apollo command you to do?
Tell me! Or did the god place it under strictest taboo?

ORESTES

I'll tell you. This was how my many troubles began.
Those terrible things with our mother I can't talk about.
Once they'd been done I was driven out, hounded
by Furies behind me to where Apollo intended,
that is to Athens to give justice to the unnamed goddesses.
There is a holy court there which Zeus set up for Ares
because of some pollution he had on his hands.
At first when I went there no one would have me
being, as I was, so loathed by the gods.

Those who felt some compassion allowed me provision
at a solitary table but beneath the same roof.
They saw to it I was silent and not spoken to
so I could have my food and drink apart from them.
Each filled his own wine bowl with a measure of Bacchus
and took pleasure from it. I suffered in silence and tried
to ignore them without confrontation
sighing great sighs, his own mother's assassin.

When I came to the hill of Ares to stand trial,
me on one platform, the eldest Fury on the other,
speaking in turn about my mother's murder
and Apollo preserved me by the witness he bore.
Athene's raised arm made the vote equal
and I left acquitted after my trial for murder.
Those Furies who settled there, convinced of the
    judgement,
marked out their sanctuary next to the court.
But those unpersuaded by the sentence pronounced
hounded me ceaselessly in endless wild wanderings,
till I went back to the shrine of Apollo at Delphi
and cast myself down there, forswearing all food,
and swore that I'd cut short my life and seek death,
if Apollo who destroyed me won't save me now.
Apollo speaking from his gold tripod told me
to come here and take the sky-fallen statue
and set it up again in the country of Athens.
So come, help me to grasp the salvation he offered.
If we can get hold of the goddess's image,
once free of my Fury-sent fits I'll convey you
in our many-oared ship back home to Mycenae.
My love, dearest sister, save me, save our house.
All's lost for me and the family of Pelops
If we can't lay our hands on the goddess 's image.

CHORUS

Some hideous divine venom has erupted
against the brood of Tantalus, grief after grief.

IPHIGENIA

Since before you came here I'd been determined
to get myself to Argos to clap eyes on you, brother.
I want what you want to free you from suffering.
I feel no more hatred for the father who killed me
and want to put our sick, broken house on its feet.
That way I'll be delivered from slaughtering you
and save our house. But we can't escape from the goddess
or the king when he sees the pedestal stripped of its image.
How will I be spared death? How plead my case?
If only two things could happen – you take the image
and also take me on to your broad-hulled boat.
If this danger's risked we may well succeed.
If I can't manage this then I'll be finished
though you could succeed in getting back home.
I'll do all I can even if it means I die to save you.
A man a house loses is always much missed
but a woman's weak and can't count for much.

ORESTES

I won't become your killer as well as my mother's.
Her blood is enough. I want to be at one with you,
and bear the same fate whether it's life or it's death.
I'll bring you back home if I get out myself
or I'll stay here with you, and die with you here.
But hear what I think. If this wasn't what Artemis wanted
why did Apollo give me his 'prophetic instructions'
to take the goddess's image to the city of Pallas?
And allow me to gaze on you here face to face?
Putting all this together makes me hope we'll return.

IPHIGENIA

How can it happen? Escaping death, getting home,
though we've got the spirit, it's all just a dream.

ORESTES

What would you say if I said kill the king?

IPHIGENIA

Guests murder their host? An unspeakable thing.

ORESTES

If it would save us I don't see why not.

IPHIGENIA

I admire your resolve which I haven't got.

ORESTES

Then find me a place in the temple to hide.

IPHIGENIA

You think we'll escape with night on our side?

ORESTES

Darkness means deception. Truth needs the day.

IPHIGENIA

There are guards in the sanctum, we can't get away.

ORESTES

Then it's hopeless! Hopeless! What *can* save us? What?

Long pause.

IPHIGENIA

Listen to this new idea that I've got.

ORESTES

What are you thinking? I need to hear.

IPHIGENIA

Those fits you suffer! I've got an idea!

ORESTES

When there's schemes to be cooked up women are good!

IPHIGENIA
I'll tell them you shed your own mother's blood.

ORESTES
Yes, use my troubles if there's gain to be had.

IPHIGENIA
I'll say as a sacrifice you'll only bring bad.

ORESTES
On what grounds? No, I don't need you to say.

IPHIGENIA
I'll say your pollution needs washing away.

ORESTES
We can't get the statue through tales about me.

IPHIGENIA
I'll claim your cleansing must be done in the sea.

ORESTES
The statue's still where it's tended by you.

IPHIGENIA
I'll say you've touched it so it must be washed too.

ORESTES
You'll go to the seashore but tell me where.

IPHIGENIA
Where your ship's moored with its sails in the air.

ORESTES
Will you bring the image or someone you command?

IPHIGENIA
Me! It's untouchable to all but my hand.

ORESTES
And Pylades here? What task can he do?

IPHIGENIA
I'll say he's polluted the same way as you.

ORESTES

Will the king be aware or not know a thing?

IPHIGENIA

I'll tell him. I can't keep such things from the king.

Pause.

IPHIGENIA

And the rest, Orestes, you do, not I.

ORESTES

The ship with its sails spread already stands by.

IPHIGENIA

One thing more. The women here must hide what we do.

ORESTES

They're in the temple. Persuade them. That's up to you.
As a woman you can arouse their compassion.
Then everything else might work out for the best.

*Iphigenia bangs on the temple door. It opens. We hear
the Chorus humming/singing their 'halcyon bird'
chorus (page 217).*

IPHIGENIA

O dearest women,

The Chorus stops humming/singing.

                    it's you I depend on.
It's up to you whether I fare well; or ill.
And end with no country, no brother, no sister.
Let me make this the ground of all my pleading.
We are all women, well-disposed to one another,
most resolute in guarding what's our shared good.
Keep silent on our behalf and let us make our flight.
A tongue that is loyal is its own reward.
Look at us, three friends united in one fate.
And that fate is return to Greece, or die.

If I survive you'll all share my good fortune.

To each individual member of the Chorus.

You, by your right hand, you, by your cheek,
you, by your knees, I beg you each one,
and by all those you love back home in Greece,
mothers, fathers, children too, if you have them.
What do you say? Will you agree or not? Speak out.
If you spurn my plea we're doomed, me and my brother.

CHORUS
Dear mistress, think only of your safety.
For my part I'll keep silent about all that you asked . . .
Zeus be my witness.

IPHIGENIA
I hope you're rewarded for speaking those words.

To Orestes and Pylades.

Your next job is to go inside the temple.
This country's king will be here before long
to ask if you strangers have been sacrificed.

To Artemis.

Mistress Artemis, who by the glens of Aulis
saved me from my father's butchering hand,
please save me here and please save these men
or the word of Apollo will be branded a liar's.
Favour us, and leave this barbarous land for Athens.
It is not proper to live here when you have a choice
between a city that's barbarous and a city that's blessed.

CHORUS
The halcyon bird laments her fate.
She mourns her much-missed mate.
I too mourn a loved one's loss
and need for my homeland makes me pine.
If I could fly like you I'd cross

to the home in Greece that once was mine.
Over the Black Sea to rejoice
with Greek women in a true Greek voice.
And raise it in praising Artemis.
Artemis of Mount Kynthos not Crimea,
goddess of childbirth not death like this,
goddess of childbirth not death like here.

If like the halcyon, I could fly
the sun's bright pathway through the sky
and hover with my wings awhirr
over my Greek home and see her,
the happy girl I used to be
dancing with others joyfully

with girls my age, my mother too,
doing the dance we used to do,
and across my cheeks as our chorus whirls
the shadows of my tossing curls.

Enter Thoas.

THOAS

Where's the Greek woman who keeps the key of this
    temple?
Sacrificing the strangers? Has she made a start?
Are their corpses already on fire in the shrine?

*Iphigenia enters from the temple with the image of
Artemis.*

CHORUS

Here she is, master. She'll make it all clear.

THOAS

Woh! The image of Artemis is off its fixed base
and cradled in your arms, Iphigenia, why?

IPHIGENIA

My lord, stay where you are in the doorway!

THOAS
What's happened here in the temple today?

IPHIGENIA
Pollution of the sacred. (*Spits.*) I spit it away.

THOAS
What are you hinting at? Say what you mean.

IPHIGENIA
These victims you brought me. My lord, they're unclean.

THOAS
Have you some proof or is it all in your brain?

IPHIGENIA
The godess's statue turned round in disdain.

THOAS
By itself? Or was it because the earth shook?

IPHIGENIA
By itself. And closed its eyes, so as not forced to look.

THOAS
Why? Do those strangers have some sort of blight?

IPHIGENIA
Because of dire deeds they're blighted. You're right.

THOAS
Did they kill some barbarians of ours on the shore?

IPHIGENIA
No, family blood-guilt both bore from before.

THOAS
Blood-guilt? I need to know. Who was it they killed?

IPHIGENIA
Their mother! It was her blood their baleful blades spilled

THOAS
Even barbarians like us don't think that's right!

IPHIGENIA

They've been hounded from Greece, always in flight.

THOAS

And you brought Artemis out so no damage was done?

IPHIGENIA

Yes, out to the air and pure light of the sun.

THOAS

How did their blood-crime come into your ken?

IPHIGENIA

The statue's turning made me question the men.

THOAS

Greece taught you something. You've got a good brain.

IPHIGENIA

There was something in them I thought to my gain.

THOAS

News of your family you hoped they could tell?

IPHIGENIA

Yes, that Orestes my only brother fares well.

THOAS

To make you feel happy and so spare their lives?

IPHIGENIA

And my father's in Argos and, so they say, thrives.

THOAS

Your service to the goddess as priestess comes first.

IPHIGENIA

Yes, Greece destroyed me, so Greece is cursed.

THOAS

So what's to be done with these Greeks today?

IPHIGENIA

They must be dealt with in the usual way.

THOAS
So they've been sprinkled and brought to the blade?

IPHIGENIA
They've got to be purified first I'm afraid.

THOAS
What's best to do that? Fresh water or salt?

IPHIGENIA
The sea washes away all foul human fault.

THOAS
They'll be acceptable victims after the sea?

IPHIGENIA
And the sea will also work wonders for me.

THOAS
It's good then the sea washes right up to here?

IPHIGENIA
It needs to be secret. This place is too near.

THOAS
I won't pry. Do whatever it's proper to do.

IPHIGENIA
I have to cleanse the goddess's statue too.

THOAS
Yes, clean the matricide's blemish off, every trace.

IPHIGENIA
Why else lift her statue up off her base?

THOAS
You've shown proper scruple in every case.

IPHIGENIA
Do you know what I need?

THOAS
                    Give your orders to me.

IPHIGENIA

Fetter the strangers.

THOAS

Why? Where would they flee?

IPHIGENIA

Nothing Greek can be trusted.

THOAS

(*to men*)

Make sure they're tied.

IPHIGENIA

Let them bring the strangers out here.

THOAS

(*to men*)

Bring them outside!

IPHIGENIA

Cover their heads with their cloaks.

THOAS

Against the hot sun?

IPHIGENIA

Send some of your men with me.

THOAS

As good as done!

IPHIGENIA

And send men to tell the city.

THOAS

What shall they say?

IPHIGENIA

They should all stay inside.

THOAS

Out of pollution's way?

IPHIGENIA

Such things *are* polluting.

THOAS
(*to men*)
So go and declare . . .

IPHIGENIA

No one should come near.

THOAS
This shows how you care.

IPHIGENIA

For friends, most of all.

THOAS
Does that mean me too?

Pause.

The whole city thinks so highly of you.

IPHIGENIA

Stay at the temple.

THOAS
And do what?

IPHIGENIA
Find sulphur to burn
to purify the shrine.

THOAS
For when you return?

IPHIGENIA

And when the strangers come out here –

THOAS
What should I do?

IPHIGENIA

Cover your eyes.

THOAS

Not to be polluted too?

IPHIGENIA

And if I'm taking too long . . .

THOAS

Take as long as you need.

IPHIGENIA

May it go the way that I hope.

THOAS

On that we're agreed!

IPHIGENIA

Now I see the strangers coming out of the temple
with the goddess's adornments and new-born lambs
for me to cleanse all that bad blood with good,
the bright flames of torches and anything else
I prescribed for cleansing the strangers for the goddess.
I proclaim to all citizens to stay clear of pollution!
Any temple attendant keeping clean hands for the goddess,
or anyone about to enter into betrothal,
or is heavy with child, all keep your distance,
so that pollution doesn't fall upon you.

Prays.

Artemis, daughter of Zeus and of Leto,
if we can cleanse the blood taint from these strangers
and we can sacrifice to you as we should,
you'll dwell in cleansed surroundings and all will be well.
Though I say nothing more the gods know my meaning.
They know about most things, as you do too, goddess.

CHORUS

Leto's noble son Apollo,
she gave birth to him with his golden locks,
skilled on the lyre and with the bow,
born in Delos's sea-girt rocks.

From Delos he crossed to where
Dionysus dances on Parnassus,
and the mottled serpent had its lair,
the Python with monstrous hisses.

Still a babe-in-arms you killed the snake
made Delphi yours, and from below
on your gold truth-throne you make
prophecies, where Castalia's waters flow.

Because Earth loathed Apollo's theft
of her daughter's prophetic role
in Delphi's holy rocky cleft
upstart Apollo stole,

she sent men night dreams they thought true
dreams meant to undermine
Apollo's oracles, and outdo
decrees the new god claimed divine.

So off sped Apollo with all haste
to where Zeus his father lives on high,
Olympus, and with boy's arm embraced
the god's throne and begged him pacify
the Earth goddess's ire and reclaim
Pythian Delphi in Apollo's name.

Enter Messenger.

MESSENGER
Temple protectors and altar attendants
where is Lord Thoas the king to be found?
Swing open these well-bolted doors and call
the king of the country to come here outside.

CHORUS
What is it? If I might be so bold to enquire.

MESSENGER
That pair of young men, they've taken flight

through the schemes of Agamemnon's daughter.
The holy image, they've got that with them too
stored in the bowels of a ship bound for Greece.

CHORUS

Incredible! What a story! But the man that you're wanting,
the king of this country, left the temple in haste.

MESSENGER

Where was he off to? He's got to know what's happening.

CHORUS

We don't know. Run after him and find him,
so you can tell him the news that you've got.

MESSENGER

You see how untrustworthy you women are.
You've something to do with all this.

CHORUS

You're out of your mind. The strangers' escape
has nothing to do with us. Go to the king's house. Quick.

MESSENGER

Not till I find someone to tell me one thing –
Is King Thoas inside the temple or not?
Ho! Unloose the bolts, you lot inside!
Let your master know I'm here at the door
bearing a pile of pretty bad news.

Enter Thoas from temple.

THOAS

Who's raising such a din in the goddess's house?

MESSENGER

Those women were lying, shooing me off,
telling me you'd gone when you were there all the time.

THOAS

What good would it do them to tell you that?

MESSENGER

I'll explain their role after. Now hear what's more urgent –
That young woman, Iphigenia, who tends the altar
is leaving the country with those two strangers.
She's got the statue with her. The cleansing's a trick.

THOAS

What do you mean? What god led her on?

MESSENGER

She's saving Orestes, it will shock you to know.

THOAS

Orestes? Not Clytemnestra's son.

MESSENGER

Yes, and the one Artemis lined up for her altar.

THOAS

A marvel! Though marvel's a weak word for it.

MESSENGER

No time for all that. Listen to me.
Once you've got the picture, sir, you must plan
and get up a pursuit to track down the strangers.

THOAS

Tell me then. You're right. It's no easy voyage
they've started on. They won't escape when we pursue.

MESSENGER

When we made it down to the seashore
where Orestes' ship was hidden at anchor,
those of us you'd sent to keep hold of their fetters
were told to keep our distance by Iphigenia
claiming she was kindling a sacred flame for the cleansing.
So she walked behind and held the fetters herself.
That seemed a bit fishy, but we just let it happen.
After a bit, to pretend there was some rite to enact,
she started that ululation thing, screaming barbaric cries,

sorcery acting, as if cleansing a blood-guilt.
After we'd been sitting there quite a long time
we started thinking, now that they're loose
they could easily kill her and make their escape
but since we were scared to look on the forbidden
we went on sitting there not saying a word.
In the end all of us agreed we should follow
even though it had all been forbidden.
Then we saw the Greek ship fledged thick with oars
with rowers all ready with their oars on their thole-pins
and the two young men, freed of all fetters,
standing on the ship's stern. Other sailors
held the prow steady with poles, and others lashed anchors
to the cat-heads and others rushed with ladders.
They let down the sides so the strangers could board.
Now that we tumbled to their tricks, our cowardice fled.
We grabbed hold of the foreign woman, and the cables
to try to drag the oar-blades out of their sockets.
Words started flying – 'What gives you the right
to steal the images and priestesses out of this land?
Who do you think you are to smuggle her out of the
    country?'
He said, 'The name's Orestes, her brother, if you must
    know,
the son of Agamemnon, and I'm fetching
my sister, who I'd lost, back to our homeland.
We kept our hold on her though, and tried to drag her
as best we could the other direction to you.

Shows face.

Look that's how I got these fist-marks on my cheeks.
They didn't have weapons, neither did we,
the two of them launched punches and kicks at us
with gashes on our heads, or black eyes.
Then, standing on sandbanks, we wage war at a distance
and pelted the enemy with pebbles and stones.

But archers on the ship's prow shot arrows at us
so that finally we had to draw further back.
Then a sea-surge pushed the ship aground.
It made the woman afraid of the waves that were rising
so Orestes went and hoisted her on to his shoulder,
waded into the sea, mounted the ladder, and placed
his sister on the ship's deck, along with the image
of the goddess that fell down from the heavens.
Then from mid-ship a voice cried, 'You sailors from
   Hellas,
grab your oars and churn the sea into froth.
We've got the things we sailed through the Symplegades
   for,
and through the passage of the "unfriendly" sea.'
And they let out a great cheerful cry
and strike the sea and as long as the ship
was inside the harbour it made for the opening.
But around the harbour mouth, it crashed into a wave
when a sudden great wind blew and spun the ship round.
They put their strength into the struggle and prevailed
but a huge flowing wave pushed the ship back to land.
Then Agamemnon's daughter stood up and prayed:
'Artemis, save me, your priestess, take me back
to Hellas from this barbarian land, and forgive me this
   theft.
You love Apollo, your own brother, goddess,
So you'll understand that I also love mine.'
The crew all assented to that with a cry,
then put all their strength into pulling the oars.
Nearer and nearer to the rocks the ship came.
Then one of our number jumped into the ocean,
another tried to get hawsers hung from the ship.
And I was straightaway sent here to you,
my lord, to tell you what's been going on there.

Go there, take bonds and nooses with you.
Unless the swell of the sea becomes calmer

the strangers haven't got a hope they'll survive.
The lord of the ocean keeps a sharp eye on Troy,
holy Poseidon hostile to the family of Pelops,
and will put into your and your citizens' hands
Agamemnon's son, along with his sister,
condemned for forgetting the murder at Aulis
and now for betraying the goddess.

CHORUS
Poor Iphigenia, you're going to die with your brother
if you end up again in the hands of our master.

THOAS
Ho, all citizens of this barbaric land
rein your horses and gallop down to the seashore
to meet up with the wreck of the ship of the Greeks.
With the goddess's help hunt these impious men down.
Let others drag speedy ships down into the sea
so we can pursue them on the ocean and on land.
Catch them and hurl them off the rough rock face
or impale their bodies on stakes.
As for you accomplices in these doings,
you women, I'll punish you, when there's more time.
Now with all this happening I can't linger here.

LIEUTENANT
(in Athena costume)
You, soldier, stop, I need your help to wind
Me up this winch.

SOLDIER
What?

LIEUTENANT
Would you mind?

SOLDIER
I hope, sir, it's not impertinent if I say
our lives are more important than your play.

LIEUTENANT

This is an order: hoist me up high

SOLDIER

Yes, sir! But don't blame me if you die.

Begins winding. Creak. Creak.

LIEUTENANT

I swore I'd do this play.

Creak. Creak. Creak.

SOLDIER

(*shouting up*)
Is that high enough?
You're cannon fodder in that golden stuff.

LIEUTENANT

My goddess costume!

SOLDIER

It's going to shine
so that they'll see you from the Russian line.

(*To self.*)
You get some barmy buggers in the army.

Creak, creak, creak.

Is that high enough?

LIEUTENANT

Yes. Yes.

SOLDIER

(*to self*)
Bloody barmy!

We hear the Soldier running away.

LIEUTENANT

Come back! Come back! I'll need you soon. Don't run!

I'll need you to winch me down once this is done.
Dammit! Dammit! But I'm going to try
To enter as Athena do or die.

Enter Lieutenant this time as Athena.

ATHENA
Where . . .? Where are you going in your pursuit?
Lord Thoas, listen to the words of Athena.
Stop your pursuit, stop sending out this flood of forces.
Orestes was destined to come here by Apollo's decree
fleeing the rage of the Furies to bring his sister back
   to Argos
and bring the holy image to my country and finally find
relief from the troubles that have been his affliction.

*The noise of bombardment gets louder.
The Lieutenant/Athena stops.*

LIEUTENANT
Fucking Russians! Boris! Ivan! PLEASE!
There aren't any snipers in Euripi-bloody-des.

Sounds of exchanged cannon fire.

Listen!

The cannon fire gets noisier.

Listen! If it gets any worse
I'll have to get a move on with the verse!
I'll try to dodge when Ruski lead flies past
and start the speech again but twice as fast.

*Lieutenant/Athena starts the speech again at double
speed.*

ATHENA
Where . . .? Where are you going in your pursuit
Lord Thoas, listen to the words of Athena.
Stop your pursuit, stop sending out this flood of forces.

Orestes was destined to come here by Apollo's decree
fleeing the rage of the Furies to bring his sister back
   to Argos
and bring the holy image to my country and finally find
relief from the troubles that have been his affliction.
This is all said for you, Thoas. As for Orestes you're
   planning
to kill on the heaving ocean, already Poseidon,
as a favour to me, has made the sea waveless
so Orestes can sail his ship over calm flatness.
And Orestes (though not present you can hear my voice)
take your sister and the statue and go on your way.
And when you reach the god-founded city of Athens
there's a place near to Attica's furthest borders
close to the coastal crags of Carystos,
sacred to my people who call it Halai.
There found a temple with the statue inside it.
Call it after the Crimea and all the ordeals
you struggled through, wandering all over Hellas
driven to frenzy by the goads of the Furies.
Artemis will be worshipped as the Crimean.
Make this a tradition – when the festival of Artemis
is celebrated by the people make sure a sword
is held against someone's throat and some blood's drawn
in place of the sacrifice that should have been you
to keep the goddess sacred and her honour intact.
Iphigenia, you will serve the goddess
as key-keeper in the sacred meadows of Brauron.
And there you will be buried when your life has ended
and people will dedicate fine-textured garments
which women who've expired in childbirth have left.

   To Chorus.

And I also enjoin you to bring these women to Hellas
because they stuck by you in your hour of need.
Orestes, you'll return to rule over Argos,

you, who I rescued one time before
when on the Areopagus the votes came out equal.
This will be a future law that equal votes
fall in the defendant's own favour.
Now convey your sister out of this country,
son of Agamemnon. And, Thoas, hold back your fury.

LIEUTENANT
Where's Thoas? Gone! God, I'll have to try
to remember Thoas's reply.

As Thoas.

Let them go to Greece along with the statue and may
they establish it there with good fortune
These women too I'll send to fortunate Hellas
as you demand. I'll lower the weapons we're raising
against the strangers and still all my oarsmen,
since these are your wishes, Goddess Athena.
Stuck up here and somewhat scared I'll die
I don't have time for all of his reply
to me (as Athena). All you need to know
he agrees to let me (as Iphigenia) go.

Lieutenant looks down.

God, from up here on my crane it's very clear
the audience has gone. Nobody's here.
Applause won't happen when I take my bow.
Sergeant! If you're around I really need you now!
The bloke who wound me up here to this height
went off, forgetting me, to join the fight.
So here I dangle in full view of our foes
not helped by the costume that I chose.
The golden helmet and the golden gown
gives them an easy target to shoot down!
I see it in *The Times*. 'Lieutenant dies
dangling on a crane in goddess guise.'

Lieutenant is wounded.

Shit! Athena's shot! I'm bloody shot!
Athena's divine and doesn't die. I'm not!
Both Iphigenia and Athena say goodbye . . .

Breathes with difficulty . . .

Our play, somewhat disappointingly, concludes
with the usual Chorus platitudes:

'Holy Victory, keep my life in your care.
Keep putting a green wreath in my hair.'

Lieutenant dies.
   Sound of warfare increases.